For Angelina and Sandro

FRESH FROM ITALY

ITALIAN COOKING FOR THE AUSTRALIAN KITCHEN

by
STEFANO MANFREDI

with
John Newton

Illustrations by
Bridget Ohlsson

HODDER HEADLINE AUSTRALIA

First published in 1993
by Hodder Headline Australia Pty Limited,
(A Member of the Hodder Headline Group)
10–16 South Street, Rydalmere NSW 2116

Copyright © Stefano Manfredi, 1993.

This book is copyright. Apart from any fair dealing for
the purposes of private study, research, criticism or
review as permitted under the Copyright Act, no part may
be reproduced by any process without written permission.
Enquiries should be addressed to the publisher.

National Library of Australia Cataloguing-in-Publication entry:

Manfredi, Stefano, 1954–   .
    Fresh from Italy: Italian cooking for the Australian kitchen.

    Bibliography.
    ISBN 0 340 53603 9.

    1. Cookery, Italian. I. Newton, John (John Sefton). II. Title.

641.5945

Designed by James de Vries
Typeset in Bodoni
in Australia by Netan Pty Limited, NSW
Printed by Griffin Press.

CONTENTS

Preface	1
From Gottolengo to Bonegilla	5
The Kitchen	15
Classic Preparations & Ingredients	21
The Antipasto	51
Winter — June to August	59
Spring — September to November	93
Summer — December to February	123
Autumn — March to May	157
Wine	183
Bibliography	188
Glossary	191

ACKNOWLEDGEMENTS

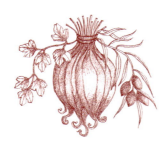

It takes a lot of people to put a book together and, looking back over the last couple of years, I would like to give thanks to those that have given 'Fresh From Italy' life.

John Newton first of all. He really took the bits and pieces and helped me put together my family's particular story. I'm greatly indebted to James de Vries whose skillful design gives the book its sense of space and elegance and allows Bridget Ohlsson's wonderful drawings to come to life.

Special tribute must be paid to Bert Hingley and Lisa Highton, his successor as Publishing Director, and all the staff at Hodder Headline who have been great under enormous pressures.

My thanks also to the staff at The Restaurant Manfredi, especially in the kitchen, who must have wondered why I was spending all those nights and days in front of a computer screen instead of being in the kitchen. The support my brother Franco gave me in organising the kitchen was invaluable and to Nicole whose work is always impeccable.

To my mother Franca especially, I thank for the inspiration and sensibility to know how good food should taste and to her mother, Angelina, my grandmother, to whom this book is dedicated.

To Julie, my wife, I owe a great debt. She has not only endured this book but has had to put up with a totally selfish individual for the last two years as well as being mother, manager and responsible for much of the style of The Restaurant Manfredi.

PREFACE

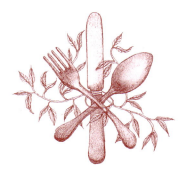

At the centre of the Italian kitchen is an invisible shrine to two principal virtues: Simplicity and Freshness.

So if I were to choose one dish that best illustrated the principles of Italian food, it would be the dish that we call *Acqua Cotta* — cooked water: when cooking water, use only the finest spring water gathered from the source.

Having said that, and having used the word 'Italian' twice in the first two paragraphs, I must warn you that this is not just another Italian cookbook of reheated classic recipes.

I am Italian. And I am a cook. But I live in Australia and, whenever I can (and that's more and more with each passing year), I seek out and use only the finest and freshest Australian ingredients.

So this book is about the way I have brought to Australia the Italian sensibility to food that I grew up with, that I absorbed as a small boy through my nose and my mouth and the pores of my skin in the kitchens of my mother and grandmother in our village of Gottolengo in Lombardy.

What we have been developing at The Restaurant Manfredi for the past ten years is a cuisine informed by the classic Italian approach to food, but relying on the best ingredients available in this country, chosen at their peak. We know that the new cannot exist without the traditional, and that tradition is constantly being nourished by the new.

This, in itself, was a revolutionary approach in an Australia with very fixed ideas of what constitutes Italian food; we knew we were on the right track when we had customers telling us that, much as they had enjoyed the meal, it was not Italian.

But the Italian *idea* of food travels well, to my mind better than any other. And it's no wonder that this preference for combining the freshest ingredients with a minimum of outside interference to preserve their tastes, aromas and qualities — not to mention the use of pasta and olive oil, tomatoes and cheese — is now as widespread in the kitchens of the world as the English language is in its classrooms. It has travelled especially well to Australia. The more I think about the two countries, the more this seems to make sense.

There are many reasons for the pre-eminence of Italian food. One is the central location of Italy in Europe, another the comparative size of the country, sprawling from the Alps to Africa, encompassing almost every imaginable climate and growing condition within its borders. How much vaster Australia (23 times the size of Italy, even including Sicily and Sardinia!), straddling Asia and the Antarctic, with growing conditions for everything from Atlantic salmon to the most exotic tropical fruit and fish.

There is also a historical explanation. The affluence and sensuality, and the heightening of artistic sensibilities, which began in the Renaissance surely spread to the kitchen: Caravaggio was as concerned with the quality of his asparagus as he was with the quality of his canvas.

And now we're witnessing an Australian renaissance in food. Arising from the ashes of an overcooked and often monotonous national food is the most vital new cuisine on the planet today — shamelessly and profitably plundering ideas and ingredients from neighbours and new arrivals alike; developing exceptional regional produce; and daily discovering natural riches that the original Australians knew about all along. This book is my contribution to that continuing process.

In The Restaurant Manfredi, the entire menu is changed at least every month, primarily to take advantage of food in its season: that is why the menus in this book are organised seasonally. Ripeness is all, and, although there are many foods that are now available year round, they are still at their best in their season, and better at their peak.

And, secondly, it would bore me to distraction to produce the same dishes week in week out, month in and month out. I inherit from my maternal grandmother a need to take risks with food, to experiment.

Remember that when you use the recipes in this book. They're not so much etched in stone as reminders of some of the wonderful things you can do when you apply imagination and good taste (in the strictest sense of the word) to the finest available produce.

FRESH FROM ITALY

FROM GOTTOLENGO TO BONEGILLA

There's a family photograph in one of my mother's albums of me as a small boy, perhaps two years old, leaning over the edge of the fountain in the *piazza* in the centre of Gottolengo, the small town of my birth in Lombardy, hand outstretched to cup the water cascading from its mouth.

It's a faded black and white photograph and, looking at it, you would say it shows very little. But I could write a book about that faded little photograph. It brings home to me in the sharpest detail the enormous differences between the land of my birth, and the land I've adopted as my new home.

First, the fountain, a fixture at the centre of just about every *piazza* in Italy. A fountain bubbling with spring water — mineral water we call it today and pay at least a dollar a bottle for it. Pure, laden with teeth- and bone-strengthening salts and minerals, lacking only pollution and added fluoride. And there it was, in the centre of the *piazza*, which itself was the centre of our world. Wherever the Romans went, they did two things: provide water, and plant grapevines.

The *piazza* itself says more for the differences between Anglo-Saxon Australia and Roman Italy than any number of books. A centre, a neighbourhood centre, a place of marketing and meeting and leisure and gossip and sitting in cafes listening to each other living. The *piazza* wasn't so much a public space, it was an extension of our house, a living room for the whole town.

A wide open room for living where you intersected with the lives of people you knew, whose parents you knew, whose parents' parents you knew — whose connections with you went back beyond history and, as you thought then, onward, a long way past your allotted time. When I think of Italian culture, I don't think of Michelangelo or Verdi or the Colosseum; I think of life as it has been lived in *piazzas* such as ours for almost 2500 years.

There are no cars in the photograph. Only a man on a bicycle disappearing into the distance, next to the door of the horse butcher (yes, horse butcher; there were two butchers in most Northern Italian towns, a horse butcher and an ordinary butcher; horse was not a necessity, but a delicacy). All of us had bicycles. My part of Lombardy is flat, and the bicycle and the motorcycle — big, brutal Moto Guzzis and Ducatis — were the preferred means of travel.

And there, in the distance, to the left of the long afternoon shadow of the lamp-post, looking young and stylish and cutting a *bella figura* in a dark dress with a white sailor's collar and white leather handbag, one of the finest cooks in the region, my grandmother, Angelina Pini.

I don't remember putting my hand out to take a mouthful of water from the fountain. But I do remember stealing into my grandmother's kitchen when I thought all the women of the family were looking the other way, reaching up to grab a handful of raw *tortelli di zucca*, and popping them in my mouth, the taste and smell of the sweet pumpkin and *frutta senapata* filling exploding through the comforting doughy softness of the raw pasta.

This, of course, is a Christmas memory. Christmas was a three-day feast of friends and family and talk and argument and cooking and food and sights and sounds and smells wafting from the kitchen, the fresh herbs hanging over the work-bench, the sausages arriving with my Uncle Sandro on his big black motorbike, strings of salamis and cotechini around his neck. (He was a travelling butcher and more often than not he was paid in kind, with meat and sausages which he ate or swapped for other foodstuffs.)

My mother and my grandmother and other aunts would be in the kitchen stuffing the little *tortelli* with mashed pumpkin, and preparing the *antipasti*: the *giardiniera* — the vegetables we'd pickled in the summer; boiled ox tongue with *salsa verde*; bread hot from the morning oven, drizzled with virgin olive oil from *Lago di Garda*, the best olive oil in that part of Italy and, felicitously, about an hour from Gottolengo by fast Moto Guzzi.

The main course would be perhaps *polpettone*, a breast of veal rolled and filled with a stuffing of yesterday's bread, rosemary, garlic and sage from Angelina's herb garden, tied, roasted, and finished with red wine. It may have been *lepre in salmi*, hare stewed in *vino brusco* (robust red wine) sauce with quills of cinnamon, cloves and lemon peel (page 76).

And later, when I grew up and could help by running down to the *piazza* for more bread or wine, there were more delicious smells and tastes to stop me, and tempt me to spend the change.

On every corner chestnut sellers, their charcoal braziers smoking, the aromatic nuts roasting — a paper coneful for 20 *centesimi* (100 to a lira). Or a salad of shank tendons, cooked long and slow until they were deliciously tender and gelatinous, then tossed in a salad and sold on little paper plates.

In the bakery, the *fornaio*, were more gauntlets to be run. At Christmas the *panettone*, like fruity brioches, would be piled high and fragrant.

For every season, my nose and taste buds have a memory. The months would be counted off by the appearance and disappearance of delicacies and fresh produce. Easter in Gottolengo was the time for *colombe*, little yeast cakes shaped like doves. We knew summer had started when the first peaches appeared on aunt Agnese's trees. The markets in springtime were especially seductive. The *piazza* would be full of stands selling frogs, snails and all manner of poultry and game; and sweet and succulent eels from the nearest lake, brought to market live and wriggling, then taken home and braised in white wine, sweet onions and fresh peas, served on a bed of steaming polenta. Cherries, persimmons, figs, pears and apples filled the kitchens with colour and fragrance. All these fruits, vegetables, cheeses, meats, fish, game and smallgoods were grown or processed, caught, hunted or poached within a 100-kilometre radius of Gottolengo. Food out of season was more than unthinkable: it was impossible. And as for anything foreign… practically a heresy. (Occasionally, and as a special treat, my mother would buy us bananas. This exotic fruit, she told us, smelling and tasting of the tropics, came from Africa!)

This is hard to imagine for most Australians, especially those from the cities. They don't know where their food comes from, and just about everything is always available, if at a premium price. Now, it seems to me, as part of a much larger process, we are looking at the food we eat again, and remembering how much better food tastes at the height of its season, how important it is to know where it comes from, and once again taking pride in the produce of *our* region. (In all fairness, as a Sydneysider, I have to record the ferocious and justifiable pride with which we have always regarded our rock oysters — now, alas, an endangered species.) The rise of regionality, in politics as well as food — this return to tribalism — is one of the phenomena of our times, a phenomenon that relates the fragmentation of the old Soviet Union to justifiable local pride in emerging regional food products — King Island cheeses, Tasmanian farmed salmon, West Australian anchovies.

In her kitchen, my mother, that alchemist, would take these local, seasonal, raw ingredients and transform them into meals that I still remember with longing and respect. It wasn't until I was thirteen or fourteen that I realised my grandmother and mother were exceptional cooks: until then, I thought everyone ate as well as we did.

My grandmother was also unusual in that she was an experimental cook. Of course, she had been a professional cook — she and my grandfather ran an *albergo*, a small hotel in Milan. It was renowned for its food. But it was more than that. She had supreme confidence — some would call it arrogance — in the kitchen. When Franca, my mother, says that I take after her, I recognise it as a two-edged compliment. Occasionally an uncle or my father would turn up in my grandmother's kitchen with a poor little porcupine that had been run over. She could turn the misfortune of the porcupine into a meal that almost justified its death. She would, could, and did cook anything edible. To perfection.

I absorbed all this food and, now I think about it, sensibility about food — its handling, cutting, combining of flavours, preparation and serving — from the time I could wobble into the kitchen and peer into the oven. A man in the kitchen was unusual in Gottolengo. The only time that the men interfered was in the preparation of polenta. That was, for some reason, a male ritual, one that we shall explore later in this book.

If I close my eyes and think of my grandmother now, the memory smells delicious. It was she who taught me to use my nose as other people use their eyes. A sense of smell is the good cook's most important ally. And, indeed, a full understanding of the olfactory sense may well be one of the last great frontiers of science — Lewis Thomas said that '... we might fairly gauge the future of biological science by estimating the time it will take to reach a complete, comprehensive understanding of odour.' When I take on new hands in the kitchen, the first thing I teach them is to be led by their noses.

But we must leave that little boy, his nostrils still filled with the rich odours of the food of his childhood, one hand reaching up to the old kitchen table to snaffle a handful of raw, sweet *tortelli*...

And do what film makers call a hard cut to the canteen of the Bonegilla migrant camp near Albury in Victoria, Australia. It's 1961. Bob Menzies is fighting hard to keep his Conservative coalition in power — he'll scrape in by two seats at the end of the year. Robin Boyd's *Australian Ugliness* will be published in that year — an eponymous analysis of the outward appearance of modern Australia. It's the first year in which some Aborigines, though only some, appear in a population count. Discreetly changed wording in the *Australian Official Yearbook* indicates a softening of the officially non-existent 'White Australia Policy'. And immigrants account for 73 per cent of the one million increase in the workforce since 1947. By 1971, there will be almost 290 000 Italian-born Australians, including the Manfredi family — mother, father, two sons and a daughter.

But little Stefano — now Steve — Manfredi isn't aware of any of this. He's six years old and he's standing in line in the canteen of the hostel waiting for his dinner. And he has noticed that something is missing.

Those of you who remember that time in Australia will recall it as a curiously sterile period. We scrubbed our floors and rubbed our pans and scoured our pots and polished our glasses until they shone. We were born in antiseptic hospitals, attended, not by wise old midwives and family members, but by men in masks with shining tools. My elder brother and I were born at home in Gottolengo, my younger sister in hospital in Australia. Bodily functions were somehow dirty, and perhaps eating was seen as the other end of the dirtiest body function of them all.

This meant that the food young Steve was about to eat had been prepared under the most hygienic conditions, was displayed behind glass to avoid contamination by germ-laden breath, and was served by determined women in starched white uniforms wearing rubber gloves — untouched by human hands, you may remember, was seen as something to be proud of, to boast about.

Oh, it was clean all right. But it had no smell! All I could smell was the lingering antiseptic odour of Pine-o-Cleen wafting up from the spotless floor, and the boiled cloth smell of the water the vegetables floated in.

If they were vegetables. Pallid pastel-coloured cubes — what were they? Some were vaguely carrot-coloured; others, by their absence of colour, were probably potatoes — but who knew? They had no taste. And what was even worse, no texture. None of the food had texture. Textures in real food are, perhaps subconsciously, complimentary and contrasting; think of the textures in a plate of antipasto — chewy meats, crunchy vegetables, cheeses that yield against the teeth. The little boy standing in the queue, pushing his nose — to the distaste of the women serving — against the glass that separated him from his dinner, was bewildered. He had no idea what was wrong, only an inchoate feeling that something important was missing.

Now I know what it was. We had left behind more than a country when we got off the boat from Italy and went to live in that migrant hostel: we'd left behind an entire culture. And in daily life, that culture was expressed in the preparation and eating of food. It was a feeling, touching, smelling culture. And it was anathema to our new neighbours.

Australia is a wonderful country. But we must never forget that the Australia we know now was invaded, in much the same way (with one vital difference) as Italy was invaded by the Romans. The English invaders who risked their lives getting here wanted things done their way. The difference was that the Roman way and the Italian way weren't that far apart to begin with.

But the Anglo-Saxon invaders of Australia brought everything with them, and either ignored or never noticed what was here.* It's only in the last fifteen years, for example, that Australians have begun to eat mussels and octopus. I have an Australian friend who used to catch baby octopus in Double Bay as a small boy, and sell them to 'the wogs' — that was us — for two shillings a bucket.

And now Australians are learning from their wog neighbours. The astonishing thing is, from that meeting between two cultures, the insular and the displaced regional, is growing one of the most eclectic, diverse and exciting cuisines — Bastard Cuisine would be a good name for it — in the world.

Nowadays, average Australians interested in food and wine probably know more (definitely more about wine) than their Italian counterparts. As there was no indigenous food culture here, there's nothing to be unquestioningly loyal to!

This lack of loyalty has meant that we are developing a uniquely open-minded approach to the making of wine, the blending of cooking techniques and the mixing and matching of produce.

And it all started in the ethnic ghettos of the outer suburbs of the great cities. In Cabramatta, right now, the future stars of Australian cuisine are growing up, doing what Franca, my mother, did in Blacktown in the 1960s — adapting, inventing, gathering and swapping.

---

* Another book published the year we came to Australia was Bernard Smith's *European Vision & The South Pacific*, an exploration of the conflict between European artistic conventions and the desire for an accurate portrayal of people and scenery. The corresponding book on culinary convention — 'Christmas Pudding in December' it could be called — has yet to be written.

I can still remember walking through Blacktown shopping centre with Franca and being stopped in our tracks outside a pet-food shop. There, on a tray, was a juicy slab of horsemeat. What luck! We bought it, took it home, sliced it wafer thin, soaked it in olive oil and lemon juice, cracked black pepper over it, and ate it, raw. It had been a long time since we'd had horsemeat *carpaccio*.

Walking through the paddocks that still surrounded our home in those days, we would pick wild fennel to cook with fish. What we couldn't buy, or find, we grew. And what we couldn't grow, we swapped, with our Greek, Maltese and, later, Lebanese neighbours. That's where you find the roots of Bastard Cuisine. Out there in the suburbs, in the backyards of Blacktown, in the market gardens of Cabramatta.

So it's not surprising that after graduating as a teacher and surviving a brief period as an ideological vegetarian, I decided, like my grandmother, to be a cook.

The road from that decision to The Restaurant Manfredi passes through such unlikely byways as sandwich making at the Observatory Cafe, running a vegetarian kitchen at the Sunshine Inn at Bondi, bush-cooking at Nimbin and finally, more decisively, preparing the vegetables for Jenny Ferguson at You and Me.

It was there that I noticed, for the first time, good quality local produce, and started eating around at other restaurants that were using it to pioneer this new cuisine — places like the Berowra Waters Inn and Reflections at Palm Beach.

Jenny worked in a very similar tradition to mine, only her roots were in Australia country cooking — she too had learnt at her mother's stove. It was while working at You and Me that I decided I was going to open my own restaurant.

So with my wife Julie, my mother Franca, and another partner (no longer with us) we began restaurant practice. We would borrow a friend's house for the night, and invite thirty, perhaps forty, people to dinner. We set up tables, asked our guests to come at staggered times, and handed them a menu on arrival. It was exactly like a restaurant, with one exception: no bill.

I don't know whether this was our invention or not — I haven't heard of it being done before — but as far as we were concerned it was absolutely essential. In a kitchen, timing and teamwork are essential. The analogy that fits for me is the one that compares working in a busy kitchen to running a marathon while juggling a dozen eggs. And, while all of us had restaurant experience, we wanted to make absolutely sure that when it was time for the real thing we all knew our places.

And so, in 1983, we opened The Restaurant Manfredi in what might appear to be an arrogant location — a back street in Ultimo in what was then a forgotten semi-industrial corner of Sydney. Time has changed all that. We're now surrounded by food warehouses, at the centre of a new business district, and, a couple of blocks away, is Darling Harbour.

At the time what attracted us was the low rent and the proximity to John Fairfax, the publishers of *The Sydney Morning Herald* and *The Australian Financial Review*, among others: journalists, we knew, liked to eat and drink.

We may have opened without tablecloths, without much on the wall to silence the clatter of waiters' footsteps; it may, in those early months, have looked like a staff canteen — but we did know exactly what we were doing and we knew, all of us, exactly how to do it.

The central idea was very simple. We had come from a specific cultural background. With this came an attitude to food, and skills in preparing it. Here, we found a new range of produce on which to use these skills and apply that attitude.

A case in point is our approach to two different kinds of seafood. While working on this book I was introduced by my seafood supplier, John Susman, to some tiny shellfish from Tasmania. They had never seen them before. I had, but not here. In Italy, I would have called them *vongole* — a baby clam caught in the Adriatic. We now serve them, along with Coffin Bay scallops, on a fresh tomato sauce with pesto — more or less a classic Mediterranean dish — or in a spicy soup with mussels from the same region (page 128).

John also calls me in regularly to choose from his supplies of reef fish — large flaked fish with a robust texture, like sweet lip, coral trout, red emperor and mahi mahi. These we roast, like meat, and often service with an anchovy and roast garlic paste (page 72). This combination is a recent addition to the menu, using traditional ingredients and produce which would never be available in Italy.

This is, in the original sense of the word, a radical approach to Italian cooking in this country: an approach based on cultural attitude and regional skills rather than a repertoire of variations on an 'International Italian' theme, which, unfortunately, is all too often the case when speaking of Italian food in this country.

And that is what I have tried to set down in this book. It is about our attitude to food, our response to raw ingredients, and the application of traditional skills to a unique set of circumstances.

I still feel about food much as the little boy nicking *tortelli* from his grandmother's table. It fascinates me, it excites me, and it really is the centre of my existence. On balance, I'm very pleased my mother and father decided to migrate to Australia. Because, as much as I love Italy, here I feel much more that I'm part of an important revolution in the eating and cooking habits of Australians. And, maybe I'm biased, but to me food, the kitchen and the dining table are at the heart of our civilisation.

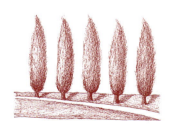

THE KITCHEN

THE KITCHEN IS MY STUDIO AND my workshop. It must be functional and attractive. It must be uncluttered and organised. It — and the tools it contains — are there to do my bidding. And, if I am to work there for days and nights on end, then it must also be easy on my soul.

And that means it should be gas-driven. Gas is a more obedient fuel than electricity; even the new halogen plates are nowhere near as responsive as gas. And then there is the very satisfying relationship we have with fire: I like to see the fire beneath the food.

Which does not mean that electricity doesn't have its place. We have an electric convection oven for baking at the restaurant and my oven at home is electric. But always gas burners on top.

I don't like microwaves. I find little use for them apart from reheating and defrosting, and even those can be easily handled with a little forethought. I do recognise their usefulness in a high turnover kitchen.

It's not that I'm against technology — the oven at home is a sophisticated German/Italian digital computer for cooking, but it does what I want it to do, and doesn't make me do things its way. You must be the master of technology, not its slave.

A food processor is a good tool, but you also need a mortar and pestle for grinding spices and a food mill for certain textures. I am wary of gadgets: as much as possible, cooking should be done by hand. Sure, I own an ice-cream maker, but only because it makes better ice-cream, especially in texture, and it's less fuss than the churn I used before.

The very beautiful thing about a well-equipped kitchen is that it contains nothing that does not have a practical significance. I can tell a good kitchen by looking at its equipment: if it is well-worn and well-cleaned, a cook works there.

Finally, the most important rule for stocking a kitchen is *not* to rush out and buy something because you've heard about it or read about it. Wait until you need it, and then buy the best quality you can afford.

Rather than describe each item needed to make the food in this book, I have had them drawn, and will only add a few notes on my own preferences in materials.

For knives, if you do not cook often, use stainless steel. Spend money on good knives, and a good sharpening steel. If you cook often, also have some carbon steel knives, especially those that need to be super-sharp, slicing tomatoes for example. But wash or wipe these knives each time you use them, use steel wool or green scouring pads once every so often, and wipe them dry.

For chopping, have a selection of large, hard-wood chopping boards — you need space when you work.

In my kitchen at home I have a stainless steel working surface with a piece of marble built into it. I prefer marble to granite aesthetically and as a material: it's semi-porous; it scratches; I like its tactile quality; it's not as cold and unyielding as granite, it's vulnerable; and for rolling out pasta or pastry it maintains a coolness that is essential. At The Restaurant we have a large piece we keep in the cool room and drag out every morning to do the pastry work (the mornings are cooler).

At home we have a set of beautiful French cast-iron pans but they're too heavy for work, so we use heavy cast-aluminium pots — they're twice the thickness of domestic aluminium pots. If we changed these pots, perhaps my next choice would be stainless steel.

For roasting, porcelain is marvellous but fragile — put it on a cold surface straight from the oven and it will crack — but it gives such an even heat. We also have heavy cast-iron roasting pans which are wonderful. Then again, something a little thinner is needed for, say, duck, because you want to get the fat off as quickly as possible and then turn it onto its skin to crisp it.

I suppose teflon is a good material, but I prefer cast-iron frying pans. If you care for them well — rub olive oil into them (our whole kitchen glistens with olive oil) — nothing sticks to them. I use pans that I've had for 15 years now.

Many of the things you will need for a well-stocked kitchen are remarkably inexpensive: stainless steel mixing bowls, wooden spoons, large stainless steel spoons that I buy in Chinatown for 95 cents each, wooden or rubber-topped spatulas.

You'll need greaseproof paper for chocolate work and muslin for straining (for example, straining almonds through the muslin into milk for almond milk).

A basic kitchen, then, consists of one stockpot, one good saucepan about 4 litres, a smaller one of 1 litre, a couple of gravy pots in cast iron with lids, and a couple of cast-iron fry pans, a skillet or two — and build up from there. Buy your hardware preferably from specialist kitchen shops, and look for places where the professionals shop.

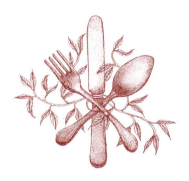

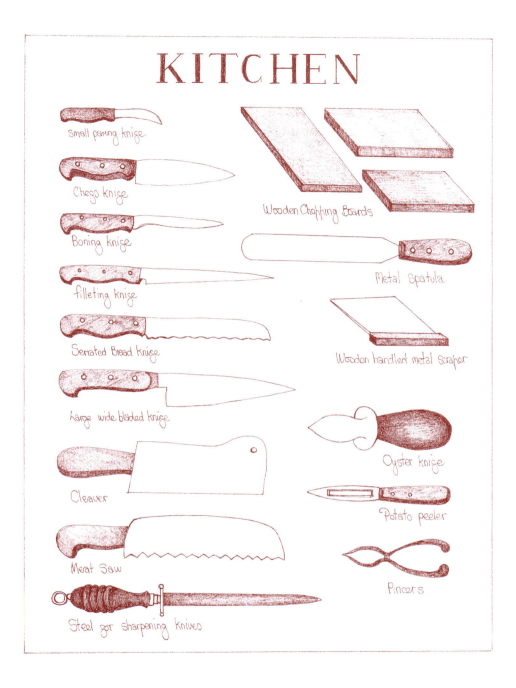

CLASSIC PREPARATIONS & INGREDIENTS

MUCH OF THE FOOD IN THIS BOOK uses the same basic preparations and ingredients. A good understanding of the principles of preparation and selection is essential.

First, the preparations: stocks, sauces, pasta and pastries. They're the things you get right before you actually start, the scales you practise over and over again so that you know them backwards and can use them to compose more complex pieces (pages 22 to 39).

And then, the prepared ingredients. These, you must understand in order to be able to buy the best — olive oil, olives, cheeses, smallgoods, for example (pages 40 to 50).

Some stocks and sauces are dishes in their own right. A classic chicken stock can be seasoned and eaten as a broth. A fresh tomato sauce can be prepared in twenty minutes and eaten immediately with pasta. More often, these stocks and sauces are used as the basis of a classic preparation — a tomato *sugo* as a base for a *ragu*; or in winter we recycle the carcasses of all the quails eaten as stock, adding white wine, carrots and leeks to make a sauce for quail and cabbage pie. (Never throw out old bones, chicken carcasses or any poultry carcasses without making stock). Or, when pan frying a veal steak, at the last minute deglaze the pan with a little veal stock and make a light sauce that is mainly juices from the pan.

In a thousand ways, the stocks and sauces described in this chapter will reappear in your repertoire.

CLASSIC PREPARATIONS

Stocks

There are three important things to remember when making stock: first, always start with cold water; second, the more you roast the bones you use, the more colour you will get in your stock (but beware — if you burn the bones, you'll get a bitter taste in the stock, so begin by roasting them lightly); finally, stock must cook long and slow.

The bones must be covered by the water — exposed bones will attract germs and possibly bad flavour — and be accompanied by the minimum of vegetables. For a 10 litre household pot, I'd use one carrot, a leek, an onion, a stick of celery and some parsley.

The vegetables used should be from the range known as aromatics (i.e. carrot, celery, onion, leek, shallot and garlic). They lend aroma, of course, and a certain complexity to the stock. I would never use parsnip, for example, or potato — nor do I use tomatoes (except in seafood stocks). Some cooks do, and add tomato paste as well to redden up the stock. I prefer the clean flavours of the aromatics alone.

Cooking times vary, depending on the ingredients used. Bones are used to provide gelatin. We cook our veal stocks for two or three days, uncovered, of course, so they reduce and intensify: veal bones, coming from young animals, are rich in gelatin-producing collagen. At the other end, chicken bones are less so, and need less time (about three hours) to extract their 'essence'. A good addition to a chicken stock is chicken feet, a rich source of gelatin.

Fish and shellfish stock take even less time (45 minutes to an hour) to make and can have herbs added to them, for example basil or even fennel in a prawn stock. Never throw out prawn heads without using them for stock first, for use, say, in a seafood risotto.

Never boil a stock. The water must be moving, not bubbling, a gentle, waving shimmer, somewhere below a simmer, and above mere warming. In that way, the essences in the bones are gently released. If you boil a stock, you are merely making murky water.

Remember that a stock should be used as a base, a background; it should never overpower the other flavours of the dish.

All stock can be made in large quantities, reduced to a concentrated essence, and frozen in individual batches for reconstitution when needed. Label each batch with its name and date.

QUAIL, CHICKEN, DUCK OR OTHER BIRD STOCK

PRODUCES 6 LITRES

Ingredients

carcasses of any birds (remove fat from ducks)
2 carrots, cut into small chunks
3 garlic cloves, whole
1 leek, well cleaned and trimmed
1 stick of celery, sliced into 1-cm sections
Italian parsley leaves
1 onion, quartered

Method

Roast the carcasses if they are raw, until they have browned slightly (20 minutes at 150°C). Put them in a pot with the carrots, garlic, leek, celery, parsley and onion and add plenty of cold, fresh water to cover everything. Simmer for about 3 hours. Do not allow to boil as this will cloud the broth. When it is ready, strain and keep aside.

PRAWN OR CRAB BROTH

PRODUCES 6–8 LITRES

Ingredients

2 kg prawn shells and heads (precooked) or 3 kg green crabs
2 celery sticks, cut into 2-cm chunks
1 carrot, cut into 2-cm chunks
2 leeks, cut into 2-cm rounds
10 ripe tomatoes, peeled and chopped
parsley, roughly chopped

Method

Place the prawns, vegetables, parsley and tomatoes in a pot. Cover with plenty of cold, fresh water and bring to a simmer. Keep simmering for $1-1^{1}/_{2}$ hours, then strain. Reduce if it is not intense enough, then season to taste.

FISH AND SHELLFISH BROTH

Ingredients

prawn shells, and bones from brook trout and reef fish
2 celery sticks, sliced into chunks
1 carrot, sliced into chunks
2 leeks, cleaned, washed and cut into thick chunks
6 ripe tomatoes, peeled and chopped
parsley, roughly chopped
salt and pepper

Method

Place the prawn shells, fish bones, vegetables and tomatoes in a large stockpot that will fit everything comfortably. Cover with plenty of cold fresh water and bring to a simmer. Keep simmering for $1-1^{1}/_{2}$ hours then strain. Reduce if it is not intense enough, then season to taste.

VEAL STOCK

With this veal stock, I add no tomato or tomato paste, or pigs' feet as has become very fashionable recently. The veal bones should have enough gelatine in them already. All I am interested in is the *essence* of the flavour and the following procedure will give you just that.

PRODUCES 1 LITRE

Ingredients

3 kg veal bones, lightly roasted to give colour (about 30 minutes at 150°C)
4 onions, peeled and halved
3 leeks, cleaned and cut into large pieces
2 carrots, peeled and cut into large chunks
3 sticks of celery, cleaned and cut into large chunks
4 cloves garlic, whole

Method

Place all ingredients into a large stock pot and cover with fresh, cold water. Bring to a simmer and keep simmering for 8 hours. Strain the liquid into a bucket. Place the bucket in the refrigerator overnight. The fat will rise to the top and solidify. In the morning it can be scooped off easily. Reduce the remaining stock until one litre remains.

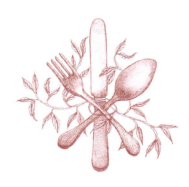

Sauces

Sauces do not have the pre-eminence in the Italian kitchen that they do in the French. For example, we don't use the sort of intense stock reductions used by the French as the basis for a sauce. Italian food is more about the taste of the ingredients, the flavour of the meat, than the taste of the sauces.

There are two basic sauce types in the Italian repertoire — the *sugo* and the *salsa**. The *sugo* is a lighter, fresher sauce including, for example, the quickly cooked fresh tomato on leek, basil and garlic, as well as the more complex slowly cooked tomato sauce with carrots, onion and celery. *Salsas* are thicker — pesto and *salsa verde* for example.

RICH TOMATO SAUCE

MAKES 2 LITRES

Ingredients

virgin olive oil
1 onion, finely chopped
1 carrot, finely chopped
1 stick celery, finely chopped
8–10 fresh tomatoes, mashed
1 clove garlic, minced
sprig basil, oregano and parsley, chopped
salt and pepper to taste

Method

Lightly fry vegetables and garlic in the oil till soft. Add tomatoes, oregano, parsley and basil. Simmer for 40 minutes till the flavours come together. Season to taste.

---

* Not to be confused with Mexican *salsa*, which tend to be chilli-hot and tomato-based.

FRESH TOMATO AND BASIL SAUCE

MAKES 1.5 LITRES

Ingredients

2 kg ripe tomatoes (the egg-shaped tomatoes are very good)
1/4 cup extra virgin olive oil
2 leeks, washed and sliced into rings
4 cloves of garlic, minced
a good handful of basil leaves, left whole
salt and pepper to taste

Method

Peel the tomatoes by throwing them into boiling water for about 30 seconds. The skin should come away very easily with the help of a small paring knife. Chop them roughly and keep them aside in a bowl.

Heat the oil in a pot, then add the leeks and garlic. Simmer gently for about five minutes until the leeks are soft. Add the chopped tomatoes and cook for as long as you like. If you want a fresh flavour then just cook for 10–15 minutes, but if you want the flavour to be more intense, then cook the sauce longer.

Add the basil leaves at the end. Season and it is ready to use.

TOMATO AND OLIVE OIL SAUCE

MAKES 1.5 LITRES

Ingredients

2 kg ripe tomatoes, peeled and mashed in a blender
half a cup of extra virgin olive oil
salt and pepper to taste

Method

Sieve the mashed tomatoes then place them in a pot. Heat the puree until it is almost at the boil (do not boil). Take if from the heat and whisk in the olive oil a little at a time until it is well incorporated. Season and allow to cool before using.

PESTO

MAKES ABOUT 250 GRAMS

Ingredients
3 cloves garlic
85 g pine nuts, lightly roasted
3 large handfuls of basil leaves
100 ml extra virgin olive oil
8 tablespoons grated parmesan cheese
salt to taste

Method
Place the garlic, pine nuts and basil in a food processor. Pulse until the ingredients start to break up. Add the olive oil gradually until it is all incorporated. Mix in the parmesan, season to taste and store in the refrigerator until it is ready to use.

Pasta

Whether pasta was introduced to Italy by Marco Polo, or was being eaten by Horace before the birth of Christ is — especially to this northern polenta-eater* — immaterial. As a cook, I recognise its genius as an ingredient; as a human being, I recognise its place in the life of humanity long before Horace or Christ.

Consider *corzetti*; to make these, you need only flour, water, eggs, and your thumb and index finger to press this small coin-shaped piece of pasta into shape. Only a human being with an opposable thumb can make this. And even if you have only these two digits, you can make *corzetti*, and pan fry them with a coating of parmesan.

You should learn how to make pasta at home. It can be done, in most cases, without a machine or any special implement. The machines, as is their habit, have usually gone too far — you can throw in the eggs, flour and water, and they will make the pasta for you — but you won't get the same result as from a machine over which you exert control.

---

* So engrained in the Italian consciousness is food that we northerners are known as *polentone* — polenta-eaters — and call our southern compatriots *spaghetti e maccheroni*.

CLASSIC PREPARATIONS AND INGREDIENTS

There is no one recipe that will give you a perfect result every time for pasta, but I will offer a specific method of making pasta that will guarantee good results, if the signposts for each step are followed.

It remains only to say that perfectly good pasta can be made with Australian wheat. Italy does not have great wheat — the best commercial pasta in Italy uses Canadian wheat. The best wheat in Italy comes from the plains of Puglia, but the wonderful pasta they make with it is due to machinery rather than wheat.

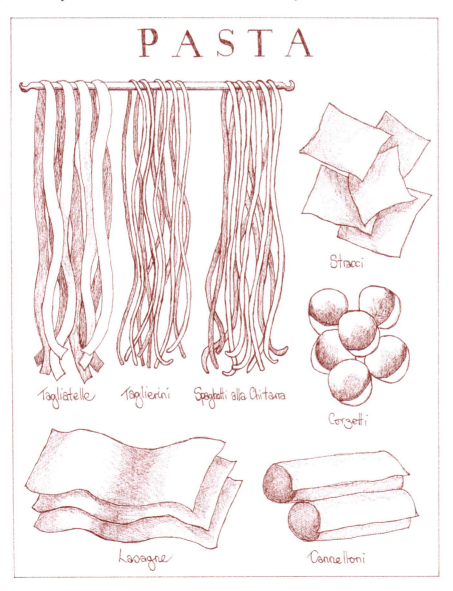

PASTA

Basic preparation

Make a well with about 500 g of plain flour. Add enough whole eggs so that, when they are worked into the flour, the dough is not sticky and not dry. Compensate by adding more flour if too sticky, or more egg if too dry.

Please note that it is easier to add more flour to a wet mixture than it is to add more egg to a dry one.

Cut the pasta dough into small workable pieces so it can be easily passed through your pasta machine. Roll it through the pasta machine till you have the desired thickness.

To colour pasta you must add a concentrated colouring agent such as saffron or squid ink.

Polenta

Polenta is to northern Italians what rice is to the Chinese, what potatoes are to the Irish — and more. There was a ritual to making polenta in my house, part of which I follow to this day, and part of which was that it was the only time my father would enter the kitchen. At some stage during the making of a polenta, he would get up and announce that it was his turn to stir the polenta. There was the feeling that if he didn't stir it then, at that particular time (it needs constant stirring, and my mother did most of it), then that polenta would not be fit for human consumption.

The other memory is etched into my psyche. My mother is turning the pot of cooked polenta onto the round wooden board with two hands. It flows out like golden lava and then, when it sets, she takes the edge of a plate, dips it in water, and makes a cross in the centre of the mound to bless it. I have no idea why, except to quote Sylvester Stallone when asked the same question after asking a priest to bless him in *Rocky V*: it looks so good. We Italians, even those who are not particularly religious, will bless anything. To the amusement of my Australian staff, I still bless the polenta.

Polenta represents one of the earliest forms of cooking — simmering ground grain in water until the mixture thickened. It could be eaten immediately, or left to cool on a slab, then sliced and transported as required.

The Latin words *puls*, usually translated as porridge, indicates the antiquity and fundamental nature of polenta as a food, for it was being made well before the Greeks taught the Romans the use of ovens*. Then, it was made with grains other than wheat, wheat generally being reserved for the tables of the rich. When maize or corn was introduced to Europe from the new world, the first shipment arrived in Venice in the early sixteenth century. In less than a hundred years, it was being grown throughout Europe and, today, the variety known as bramata, grown around Bergamo, is deemed to be the tastiest and most beautifully textured for polenta. Here in Australia, the best cornmeal for polenta is grown in Queensland.

It is really very simple to make a polenta. The main thing is to avoid lumps, which is why it must be stirred constantly over a low flame. You will easily master it with practice. Once cooked it should be cut with a string, which is drawn along under it, and then lifted to cut off a slice.

POLENTA

Ingredients

1.25 litres salted water
250 g polenta flour

Method

Bring the salted water to the boil. Add the polenta flour in a fine stream, stirring constantly so no lumps form. Keep stirring until you see the polenta come away from the sides of the saucepan. Turn down the heat to a very low simmer and cover the saucepan with a lid for 25 minutes, stirring it well every 5 minutes or so.

When it is ready, either keep it on a very low simmer to serve soft, or turn it out onto a wooden board and allow it to set.

To store polenta in the refrigerator, wrap it in a tea towel or a piece of cloth. Do not store in a plastic wrap.

* Although the mysterious Etruscans were baking bread — the ancestor of *focaccia* — long before the Romans learnt to cook.

Risotto

Italy is Europe's major rice-grower — a fact often forgotten by a world convinced that Italians eat only pasta. The most widely used Italian rice for preparing risotto is Arborio, originally grown around the town of Arborio in Piemonte. It's a big, wide-grained pearly rice, and slowly sucks up the liquid — stock — until it reaches the creamy perfection of a true risotto.

Then there are the rices of Gabriel Ferron, whose family has been milling rice near Verona since 1650. The methods of production have changed little since that time.

The rice cooked by this method is, by Ferron's own admission, 'not very good looking', but the proof, after all, is in the risotto.

Two Ferron varieties are available in Australia. Vialone Nano, classed as a 'semi-fino', because of the medium size of its grain, which has a full, delicately herbaceous flavour. And my favourite, Carnaroli, which has a larger and longer grain, and remains a little more textured on cooking as it absorbs less of the broth therefore being more *al dente*.

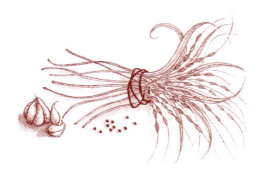

RISOTTO

Basic procedure

This procedure makes a very basic risotto using chicken or quail broth. Dried porcini mushrooms (soaked to soften them) can be added for a classic rich flavouring. Seafood risotto can be made by substituting prawn or crab stock for the meat broth and adding mussels or any other seafood. Don't add too much in the way of meat or seafood as a risotto should always be understated and dominated by the rice.

SERVES 4 AS A FIRST COURSE

Ingredients

350 g Arborio rice
1 onion, thinly sliced
1 clove garlic, minced
60 g butter
2 tablespoons extra virgin olive oil
100 g parmesan, grated
2 litres chicken or quail broth (boiling) (page 23)
salt and pepper to taste

Method

In a saucepan heat the olive oil and half the butter. Add the onion and the garlic and fry gently until the onion is transparent. Add the rice and fry gently for 2–3 minutes, stirring with a wooden spoon.

Now add a ladle or two of the boiling broth. As the simmering rice absorbs the broth, add more with the ladle. Repeat this procedure until the risotto is cooked.

I like mine a little undercooked, *al dente*. Remember that it will keep cooking even after the risotto is taken off the heat.

When the risotto is cooked fold in the parmesan and the rest of the butter. Season and serve hot.

Pastries

People who care about these things more than I do are adamant that all the basic pastries listed in Larousse as being of French origin were taken to France by cooks attached to the courts of Caterina de Medici, who married Henry II of France, and Maria de Medici, the second wife of Henry IV. Others loudly insist this is nonsense. Who cares? Whoever is to blame for these wonderful inventions — *pasta soffiata* (choux pastry), *pasta sfoglia* (puff pastry) and *pasta frolla* (shortcrust pastry) — is of interest only to historians. French or Italian, they are as pleasing to the *gusto* as they are disastrous to the *figura*.

PAN DI SPAGNA (SPONGE)

Ingredients

8 eggs
160 g icing sugar
160 g plain flour, sieved
60 g melted butter

Method

Beat the eggs and sugar together over a low flame until they are just warm.

Take away from the heat and beat until they triple in volume. Fold in the flour and the butter.

Pour into two 18 cm x 25 cm sponge tins and bake for 18 minutes at 180°C.

PASTA MADDALENA (GENOISE)

Ingredients

6 egg yolks
75 g caster sugar
6 egg whites
150 g caster sugar
80 g plain flour, sifted

Method

Cream the yolks and the first amount of caster sugar until they are thick and fluffy. Whip the egg whites and second amount of sugar together until they form soft peaks. Now fold the two mixtures and the flour together.

Spread onto two baking sheets and bake in a preheated oven at 180°C till just *under*cooked.

PASTA SOFFIATA (CHOUX PASTRY)

Ingredients

250 ml water
60 g butter
250 g flour
4 eggs
pinch salt

Method

Bring the water, butter and salt slowly to the boil. Remove from the heat, sift in the flour and work mixture over moderate heat until a thin crust forms on the bottom of the saucepan. Transfer mixture to a clean saucepan and rest for two minutes.

Add eggs one at a time, beating each in thoroughly with a wooden spoon before adding the next.

Pipe the mixture into 12 small mounds on a baking tray and sprinkle lightly with water before baking in preheated oven at 220°C for 20 minutes. Cool on a cake rack.

PASTA FROLLA (SWEET SHORTCRUST PASTRY)

Ingredients

175 g plain flour
1/4 teaspoon baking powder
pinch salt
65 g caster sugar
125 g chilled butter
1 egg yolk

Method

Mix the flour, baking powder, salt and sugar. Work in the butter and the egg quickly. Rest in refrigerator for at least 1 hour.

Roll out onto a 26-cm pie tin and rest again for 1/2 hour before using for a sweet shell.

PASTA FROLLA PARMIGIANA (PARMESAN SAVOURY SHORTCRUST PASTRY)

Ingredients

250 g flour
125 g butter
60 g parmesan, grated
1 whole egg

Method

Bring all the ingredients together in the food processor with a few short bursts. Shape into a log, cover with cling wrap and refrigerate until needed.

This pastry can be used for a savoury shell, as in the Jervis Bay Oyster Tart (page 75).

PASTA SFOGLIA (PUFF PASTRY)

For the dough

Ingredients

the prepared dough (above)
500 g plain flour
125 g unsalted butter
250 ml water
juice of 1 lemon

Method

Form a dough by blending all the ingredients. Wrap and cool until it is firm.

For the pastry

Ingredients

375 g unsalted butter, cut into slices

Method

Roll the dough out into a rectangle and place the butter slices across half the area. Lay the butter slices along the same way and fold the other half of the dough over the butter, enveloping it. Turn the envelope of dough a full 90 degrees.

Roll the dough to form a rectangle again. Now fold the outside edges of the rectangle into the centre and the whole is then folded again in the centre, like a book. This is a half turn.

Repeat the procedure, rolling the dough to a rectangle, always towards the open edges. Repeat the 'book fold' and a full turn is completed. Rest dough in the refrigerator for 20–30 minutes.

It is essential that a neat rectangle with straight edges be maintained throughout the procedure. Repeat until the pastry has been through three full turns. Refrigerate until needed.

CREMA INGLESE (RUNNY CUSTARD)

MAKES 1 LITRE

Ingredients

600 ml single cream
5 egg yolks
175 g sugar

Method

Heat the cream but don't boil. Whisk the egg yolks and sugar until the mixture forms a ribbon.* Add the heated cream and keep whisking until the mixture is smooth. Place on a low flame and stir continuously with a wooden spoon until the custard is thick enough to coat the spoon. This should take 10–15 minutes. Transfer immediately to a bowl and allow to cool.

Can be used to accompany poached fruits such as figs or peaches, and is truly wonderful with pastry of any kind.

CREMA PASTICCERIA (PASTRY CREAM)

MAKES 1.5 LITRES

Ingredients

5 egg yolks
185 g sugar
85 g plain flour
2 cups milk
2 teapoons vanilla extract or 1 vanilla bean (scraped)

---

* When the yolks and sugar are beaten, they become pale, and when the whisk is drawn across the surface and lifted, the beaten mixture falls and resembles a ribbon.

Method

Whisk the egg yolks and the sugar together until the mixture is thick and forms a ribbon.* Sift in the flour and whisk until it is well incorporated.

Heat the milk with the vanilla till it is almost boiling. Add the milk a little at a time to the egg mixture and whisk until it is blended.

Place in a saucepan and cook at moderate heat, whisking continuously for 2–3 minutes until it bubbles and thickens like a *maionese*. Turn down the heat and keep whisking for another minute or so.

Transfer immediately to a cool bowl and cover the surface of the cream with plastic wrap to prevent a skin forming.

A RICHER CREMA PASTICCERIA

Ingredients

500 ml cream
500 ml milk
200 g sugar
12 egg yolks
80 g cornflour

Method

Add the cornflour to the egg yolks then proceed as for crema inglese (p.38). Cool, then fold the pastry cream into whipped cream in equal quantities.

This makes a richer, creamier pastry cream and can be used for filling tarts before topping with fruit or for filling pastries.

---

* See explanation, page 38

PREPARED INGREDIENTS

Before anything else, you need a good merchant. When buying such things as olive oil, vinegar, parmesan cheese, your merchant must be an expert on quality, and have the generosity of spirit to allow you to taste before you buy. In this way, you learn the difference in taste and quality between, say, an olive oil to be eaten raw over salad, and a good cooking oil.

Naturally, the very best quality of any of these ingredients is expensive — a good Italian virgin olive oil can cost up to $50 a litre, a real balsamic vinegar is among the most expensive liquids on earth. But then, the difference between ordinary food and wonderful food is, to a great extent, dictated by the quality of the ingredients used in its preparation.

Olive oil

It may be that, as an Italian, I am biased, but we use no oil other than olive oil either at home or at The Restaurant Manfredi. There's nothing like it. But within the general category there are several grades of varying quality, with different uses.

From August 1993, Australian labelling regulations superseded any European regulations regarding the naming of olive oils. Here is what the names on the labels mean:

Virgin olive oil is, quite simply, olive juice, extracted from the fruit of the olive tree solely by mechanical or other physical means without the use of heat. There are two types of virgin olive oil.

Extra virgin is virgin olive oil of absolutely perfect taste and odour and an intense fruity flavour, with maximum acidity (in terms of oleic acid) of 1 per cent; and there is *virgin olive oil*, allowed a maximum acidity of 3 per cent.

The Australian regulations discourage the use of the term 'cold-pressed' because they believe the term has no meaning, as most oils today are extracted by centrifugal force rather than pressing. There are, and will always be, Italian oil makers who will cold press their oil in the traditional manner — that is, pressing the olive fruit between stones to extract the oil.

Refined olive oil is obtained by refining oil that has been extracted from the fruit of the olive tree solely by mechanical or other physical means, but which is not considered acceptable for consumption without further processing or blending because of its acidity or 'off-taste'. This refining is usually done by distillation, often using petroleum by-products. Refined olive oil is without specific colour, odour or taste. To restore the distinctive flavour, colour or aroma, it is blended with a small percentage (5 per cent is usual) of virgin oil. These oils can make perfectly acceptable cooking oils.

As for quality, my prejudice would again have it that the finest oils are Italian, especially those from the north: Liguria, Umbria, Tuscany. But the French, the Spanish and the Greeks also make some very fine oils, each with its distinctive national and even regional taste characteristics. It may be that you will prefer a particular French or Spanish oil. Your merchant will help you to acquire a palate, and to recognise the differences.

Generally speaking, oils from fruit grown in warmer climates, southern Italy for example, will be more robust, full-bodied and peppery; those from the north, finer, suaver, and lighter in taste. Also generally speaking, French oils, usually from Provence, are sweeter, with more floral overtones in the taste.

Recently, Australian olive oils have come onto the market*, some very good indeed. At the time of writing I have just tasted the latest Joseph oil from Primo Estate in South Australia, and it is the best Australian oil I have tasted so far.

In the kitchen you will need at least two oils, perhaps more: a cooking and deep frying oil, that is to say a refined olive oil, and a good quality extra virgin for eating raw on, say a fennel salad. Then, perhaps a third oil, a big, gutsy extra virgin for mixing in with a puree of Jerusalem artichokes or whisking through roast garlic as a garnish for grilled fish.

Three of my favourite Italian oils are the Mancianti 'Affiorato' from Umbria, a complex, elegant oil with ample body — perfect for a delicate salad (crab, for example) where it is to be a part of

---

* Olive oil has been pressed in Australia, at various times and places (perhaps earliest in South Australia) since the 1850s. Mostly, however, it was used for medicinal purposes.

the overall taste. Laudemio, from Antinori, in the hills of central Chianti, is a robust, spicy oil with peppery flavours (this is one of the warmer parts of Tuscany). I would use this to dress a rare, aged roast beef. And from Le Marche, on the Adriatic coast of Central Italy, comes a particular favourite, Zaccagnini, fine light and almost lemony. I would use this to cook delicate-flavoured fish (such as whitebait) or to dress a poached cod with a little lemon.

Cheeses

When first we came to Australia, there was cheddar. That has been one of the biggest changes. Today we produce literally hundreds of cheeses, across all of the categories. Many of the cooking and eating cheeses we use are Australian, although there is the class of cheese known as *grana*, whose most famous member is Parmesan, because it comes from the province of Parma. When made for the table, the cheese from this region is called Reggiano. In our kitchen we use *Grana Padano* from Lombardy.

Grana is so called because it is a fine-grained cheese, used in cooking because it does not turn into elastic threads when it melts. A good *grana* improves — and is more expensive — with age, and indeed the aging process is as carefully shepherded as the aging of a fine wine.

It's a cow's milk cheese that should be pale yellow, firm and covered with tiny holes. Beware the dry, white, crumbling Parmesans mouldering, uncared for, on delicatessan shelves.

Australia now makes very good mozzarella and *bocconcini* — not, as originally, with buffalo milk, but then neither are most of those imported; there's a very good Tasmanian gruyere, so good you can grate it on pasta; and an excellent mascarpone, a fresh sweet cheese, a perfect cheese to make with the high-fat Australian milk.

Coming from the north of Italy, I rarely use pecorino, or *sardo*, both sheep's milk cheeses and good on pasta or for cooking, but these are readily available in Australia, as are most Italian cheeses now. And as the Australian product improves, we find ourselves using it more and more, on the table and in the kitchen.

Prosciutto

The best prosciutto comes from Parma because, folklore would have it, the pigs are fed on the whey from the production of Parmesan cheese. (Good prosciutto is also made at San Daniele.)

Unfortunately, unless you leave Australia, you will never taste it. Current legislation (and there is a possibility it will change) prohibits the import of 'raw' meat products. They are raw only in that they are not heated. Prosciutto is lightly salted for 30 to 60 days, washed, hung in a warm draught for a week, then on hooks in the cool mountain air for a further 6 to 7 months.

Prosciutto is made in Australia — reasonable ones in Victoria and South Australia — but as yet nowhere near the quality of the Italian product.

The problem is that we do not raise pigs specifically to make prosciutto. The presence of hormones in the flesh often means that the bone won't take the curing salt. The butcher who used to make my prosciutto, and stopped, said that 30 per cent of the legs he tried to cure would rot from the inside. The hormone inhibits the ability of the ham to age properly. Once more, produce is of prime importance in determining product quality.

Vinegar

Red wine vinegars are the most used in our kitchen, and I always substitute apple cider vinegar for white wine vinegar, especially in salad dressings. It has a delicious flavour because it's alkaline rather than acidic.

Which leaves the king of vinegars — balsamic — about which much has been written and many lies have been told.

The Traditional Balsamic Vinegar of Modena is made from the cooked must from sweet trebbiano grapes (the grapes used to make Lambrusco), matured by a long and slow vinegarisation process through natural fermentation in large casks of certain types of wood — cherry and chestnut are two. As the vinegar ages, and shrinks in quantity, it's decanted into progressively smaller casks, so that the smallest cask contains the oldest vinegar. Commercial balsamic vinegar is usually at least three years old, and the older it is, the more expensive, with the really ancient 100-year-old vinegars selling for around $1000 a litre.

Good balsamic should be dark brown, with a syrup-like consistency, a complex, sharp and pleasantly acid nose, and a full, rich, complex flavour.

Olives

To pluck a piece of fruit from the olive tree and bite into it is to realise the level of human culinary ingenuity: nothing tastes worse. Yet, paradoxically, very few foods taste better than a well-cured olive. To rid the olive of the bitter and poisonous glucoside abundant in its flesh, we had to develop the time-consuming processes that cure it.

There are five basic curing techniques: soaking in olive oil for several months; water curing; brine curing; dry curing in salt (sometimes also rubbed with oil); and lye-curing.

Most commercial olives are cured in lye (caustic soda) because all other methods take from one to six months, and lye-curing takes only a few days. These commercially cured olives lose most of their fruit flavour, tasting mainly of salt and acid.

A variation on all these techniques is to crack the olives and cure them in oil or brine, which speeds up the process a little. Such olives rarely leave their country of origin.

Good olives are available in Australia from Italy (try to find the small and luscious Ligurian olives), Greece and France. Most Spanish olives sold here are commercially cured. Australia is now producing some excellent olives — we serve them oil-cured from South Australia in The Restaurant Manfredi.

When buying olives in bulk, remember to take your own jar and store them in their mother brine or oil. They should keep,

out of the refrigerator, in a cool spot, for weeks, perhaps even months.

When cooking with olives, if they're very salty, and you don't want the olive taste to take over — put them in at the end. If you want the dish very 'olivey', put them in at the beginning but compensate for the salt. Remember that black olives have more flavour to add, and that green olives are milder. When braising a fish, use green olives with subtle fish like cod, or black olives with oily fish like sardines, tuna or mackerel.

Sausages, salami, pancetta

So far, I have not found any Australian-made Italian-style cured salami or *pancetta* of the same quality as the Italian product. And, as long as the ban on imported uncooked meat products lasts, one of the small prices we pay for living in Australia is doing without sausage, at least for now.

There are, however, very good examples of *salsicce* and *cotechino* available. Their manufacture involves a different part of the animal, and is not as reliant on the method of its raising.

RAW INGREDIENTS

Offal

Ever since I can remember, both my mother and grandmother prepared classic offal dishes for their families. In the cold northern winters, large bowls of steaming tripe braised in wine were brought to the table. There was not a hint anywhere of that bland, white sauce that is solely responsible for many people's aversion to the stomach of oxen as food. Instead, the honeycomb-textured tripe was braised with aromatic vegetables over a long, slow heat until it was barely able to hold itself intact, finished by adding fresh, sweet garden peas and accompanied by slices of golden polenta.

On warmer days, the insides of chickens — hearts, livers, giblets — and even their crests and wattles were carefully cleaned and trimmed ready to be the main ingredients in a *ragu*. Its aroma would waft out into the street and was guaranteed to bring us kids running.

We were taught from a very early age to appreciate all foods; not just the special, but the humble foods were prepared and respected in such a manner that their flavours were indelibly cast in our memory. It's the interaction of culture, raw ingredients and, often, necessity that inspires the creativity that leads to such classic dishes.

For example, in Lombardy, a wonderful salad of calf's feet was made by simmering the feet in water with celery, carrots and onions until they were quite tender. After setting them aside to cool, they were boned, and the gelatinous remains sliced into thin strips. Some finely sliced raw onion was added and the salad was dressed with good olive oil and vinegar, then tossed with *rucola* or radicchio. This salad can still be bought in the food shops in Milan.

Closer to home, our appreciation of offal is in its infancy, with most Australians unable or unwilling to experiment with it. Where did this negative attitude come from? It's partly a modern distaste for eating anything too closely resembling the animal it came from, and partly a snobbish resistance to what is seen as 'inferior' cuts of meat ('We only serve prime cuts here,' a Sydney butcher once told me proudly).

Tripe might be easy to get, but calf sweetbreads, veal kidneys and veal brains are almost entirely exported in the belief that no domestic market exists. Even our up and coming young cooks seem to be at a loss when trying to devise offal dishes for their restaurants. They'll usually opt for a prime cut of meat and take the easy way out. Surely the real art of cooking consists of the ability to prepare not just the obvious and delicious, but also to transform the humble and ordinary. One of the most memorable dishes I've ever eaten was a pig's ear stuffed with sweetbreads, tongue and mushrooms, crumbed and baked in the oven until crisp. This was a product of the Berowra Waters Inn team, and I guess it would make many people happy.

The *Macquarie Dictionary*, the custodian of Australian English, defines offal as '... the inedible parts of a meat carcass after slaughter, excluding the skin... the discarded by-products of a manufacturing process... anything worthless or discarded; rubbish'. An extraordinary series of definitions, which means the Australian meat industry is making money out of exporting what is defined in the dictionary as 'rubbish' to France and Germany!

We should make an effort to forget this notion of offal as second-rate food and begin to appreciate the delights and pleasures of these neglected products. In the wide world of human eating habits, this aberrant Australian viewpoint (it exists in mainstream America also), is a minority one: in the great food cultures of Europe and Asia, offal is regarded as a delicacy and, given the way Australian cooking is evolving, we should be turning for inspiration to Italy, France and our closest neighbours.

Fish

In Australia, we're blessed with both abundance and variety in our choices of fish and seafood and, compared to the rest of the world, it's inexpensive. As well as being the last great hunted resource (even though more and more fish are being harvested), it's also the last great adventure for the intrepid cook: there are still things being pulled out of the sea that have never been cooked!

But the sad fact is that very few home cooks can be bothered with — or are frightened of — experimenting with the more interesting fish. I don't mean taking home prepared fillets of perch, but buying and cooking a whole red emperor, or even cleaning and cooking a large octopus.

With the help of my fish merchant, John Susman, I've arranged the more available and best-tasting Australian fish into four categories based on cooking techniques. Those categories are oily, firm-fleshed, white and broad-flaked fish. Of course a fish may be at once oily and broad-flaked, like kingfish and salmon, or firm-fleshed and oily, like tuna and mackerel. But I hope this method will be of some help in confronting a fish shop or fish market full of fish that you have never laid eyes on, let alone tried to cook. Just follow the general principles and learn from your mistakes.

Oily fish

Anchovy	Kingfish	Bonito
Sprat	Tuna	Trevally
Whitebait	Spanish mackerel	Mahi Mahi
Sardine	Wahoo	Pilchard
Rock cod	Mullet	Mangrove jack
Catfish	Tommy ruff	Moonfish

Poachable
| Atlantic salmon | Brook trout |
| Ocean trout | Rainbow trout |

Cooking the oily fish

Ideal for grilling, barbecuing, searing or pan frying, in fact any kind of cooking involving high heat and oil. For example, trevally, a common fish whose flavour I love, can simply be rolled in chopped herbs (parsley, fennel, basil and thyme) and pan fried whole in olive oil.

The smaller fish in this category — the anchovies, sprats, whitebait, sardines and pilchards — can also be deep fried. Anchovies or sprats (often sold in Australia as whitebait, although real whitebait are no larger than a matchstick) can be dusted with flour, deep fried in olive oil and served simply, with wedges of lemon.

Under the heading 'poachable' in the list is a subgroup of oily fish, the salmons and the trouts. Poach salmon steaks, or a whole salmon if you have a fish kettle, in a court bouillon or a light fish stock, and serve the fish with a tasty accompaniment like pesto, *salsa verde* or a garlic *maionese*.

It may surprise you to know that the Japanese are not the only ones to eat raw fish. The Italians also love raw tuna and swordfish, for example, thinly sliced and dressed with nothing more than extra virgin olive oil, salt, pepper and perhaps a little lemon.

CLASSIC PREPARATIONS AND INGREDIENTS

Firm-fleshed fish

| Swordfish | Deep sea bream | Tuna | Shark |
| Leatherjacket | Spanish mackerel | Moonfish | Garfish |

Cooking the firm-fleshed fish

You'll notice a bit of cross-over in this list. There are some oily fish that are firm-fleshed, which enables you to braise them, in addition to using the methods for treating oily fish. For example, take some tuna or swordfish steaks, place them in a saucepan with chopped ripe tomatoes, garlic, onion, basil and olive oil, simmer covered until the fish is cooked, and then pull the flesh apart with a fork and serve it one of two ways: cold as part of an antipasto, or hot over pasta.

This kind of braising can also be done with the salmons from the oily fish group.

White fish

Schnapper	Bream	Gurnard
Redfish	Whiting	Flathead
Garfish	Wrasse	John Dory
Ocean perch	Silver Dory	Pearl perch

Cooking the white fish

These fish have the most subtle flavour and the least amount of oil in our listing. They're probably also the most versatile in terms of cooking. They can be pan fried or deep fried whole. Garfish can be roasted in the oven (page 136), poached or braised, and this is the type of fish that is usually wrapped in a batter and deep fried.

A very simple batter is flour and water mixed into a paste, but don't mix all the lumps out of it. Those lumps contain air, and when they hit the hot oil they cause minor controlled explosions, and you get those delicious stalactites of batter.

Broad-flaked fish

Blue eye cod	Parrotfish	Red emperor
Coral trout	Barramundi	Murray perch
Skate	Jewfish	Grouper
Red-throated emperor	Sweetlip	Red mullet

Cooking the broad-flaked fish
This class of fish will take searing in a pan, and finishing off in the oven, like a piece of meat, and will generally steam and poach well. For instance, take a chunk of red emperor about 3 cm thick, sear it on both sides in olive oil, then cover it with chopped wild fennel. Place it in an oven preheated to 200°C for about 7 minutes. Take it our and serve with roast garlic, or a peperonata (page 129).

This group includes the reef fish — red emperor, red-throated emperor, coral trout, sweetlip, grouper and parrotfish, mostly coming from north Queensland or the northern part of Western Australia. They grow to considerable size very quickly, like tropical plants.

Finally, as is the case with wine, it helps to cultivate a friendly and knowledgeable merchant to ensure a good supply of interesting fresh fish and seafood — and that means a fishmonger who buys personally and daily from the nearest fish market.

For example, in the Sydney fish market, there's a special area known as the mixed catch bay, which often has for sale small quantities of more interesting fish. Ask your friendly fishmonger to check out this area or its equivalent near you for anything special or unusual.

And, finally, a good fishmonger will be able to help you by cleaning and preparing octopus and squid, and procuring raw lobsters or regional specialities, like Coffin Bay scallops.

THE ANTIPASTO

The word antipasto means, literally, 'before the meal' and in Italian gastronomy includes a vast array of appetisers limited only by the imagination of the cook. The antipasto has, for many centuries, been used to tantalise and excite the palate in antici-pation of the meal to come, or just as something to snack on between meals.

It can be laboriously elaborate or simple and understated, but the antipasto should always have seduction as its goal. Everyone gets a taste of many flavours, colours, textures and smells but only a little of each so that the anticipation of what is to come is dramatic.

The antipasto can consist of anything, from pastry and roast meat to seafood and fruit such as melon or fig. As long as the produce is fresh and in prime condition, the cook has merely to preserve and marry flavours.

Here are some of the ideas that we use at The Restaurant Manfredi.

BORLOTTI BEANS

Shell the fresh beans. Place them in a pot, cover with cold water. Bring to the boil and simmer until tender but not overcooked. Drain excess water, dress with olive oil, season, add chopped parsley and garlic.

GREEN BEANS

Bring salted water to the boil. Cook beans till '*al dente*'. Drain and dress as for borlotti beans.

DRIED TOMATOES

Choose ripe, full flavoured egg tomatoes. Slice in half from top to bottom and place, cut side up, on a mesh oven rack. Salt the tomatoes lightly, using good quality coarse salt.

Place in the oven (a convection oven is best) with just the pilot light, if gas, or on the lowest setting, if electric. Usually drying will take at least 10 hours. You will have to monitor the tomatoes carefully until you get to know your oven. They should still be moist.

Store the dried tomatoes under olive oil until needed.

ONION AND BASIL FRITTATA

MAKES ONE LARGE 20-CM FRITTATA

Ingredients

7 eggs
a handful of parmesan
a few fresh basil leaves
olive oil
1 onion, chopped into rounds
salt and pepper

Method

Crack eggs into a bowl. Beat lightly, then add parmesan and basil. Heat oil in a 20–25-cm iron skillet pan, add the onions and cook until soft. Turn up heat, then add egg mixture and cook. Lift the edges as they cook with a spatula.

Turn the frittata and cook the other side. Allow to cool then slice wedges for the antipasto.

FRIED SAFFRON CORZETTI

Corzetti means literally 'little golden coins'.

Ingredients
basic pasta dough coloured with 1/2 teaspoon saffron thread
grated parmesan cheese
olive oil

Method
Once the dough is made, take small pieces the size of a thumbnail off the large lump. Keeping your fingers well floured, press each piece onto the work surface with your thumb so that it is roughly round.

Cook the *corzetti* in an abundant amount of rapidly boiling salted water until they are *al dente*. Drain them and dress them with some olive oil so that they don't stick to one another. Mix in a generous quantity of grated parmesan cheese.

Heat a little olive oil in a pan and toss in the *corzetti*, till golden. Add them hot or cold to the antipasto.

ROAST TUNA WITH OLIVES AND ONIONS

Ingredients
choose a fresh 2-cm thick tuna steak
1 medium onion, thinly sliced
a handful of pitted olives
2 cloves garlic, thinly sliced
some basil leaves
2 ripe tomatoes, chopped
olive oil
salt and pepper

Method

Sprinkle the bottom of a baking dish with olive oil. Place the tuna in the middle and all the other ingredients mixed up around it. Sprinkle with more olive oil and season. Place in a moderate oven for about 15 minutes. The tuna should be pink in the middle.

Allow to cool, then with a fork separate chunks of tuna from the steak and serve.

FENNEL AND OLIVE SALAD

Choose nice fat fennel bulbs and trim away the coarse outer layers. Finely slice the fennel and add your favourite olives. Dress with good olive oil, season and sprinkle with some chopped dried tomatoes.

CALAMARI FILLED WITH PROSCIUTTO AND CAPSICUM

SERVES 8–10 AS PART OF THE ANTIPASTO

Ingredients

2 roast red capsicum with the skin removed and sliced
4 pieces finely sliced prosciutto
1/4 cup basil leaves
2 diced bocconcini (fresh mozzarella balls)
4 fresh cleaned calamari tubes
1/2 cup fresh tomato sauce (page 26)

Method

Mix the capsicum, prosciutto, basil and *bocconcini* together. Fill the squid tubes with this mixture. Close the ends with toothpicks. Put some tomato sauce in a baking dish and place the squid in the sauce. Cook in a moderate oven until the squid is tender (about 15 minutes). Allow to cool then slice into bite-size pieces.

THE ANTIPASTO

SLICED VEAL SHANK

Ingredients

1 veal shank, trimmed of excess fat and skin
2 carrots, cut into chunks
1 onion, cut into quarters
2 sticks celery, cut into 2-cm lengths
1 leek, cleaned and trimmed
some shallots
a large handful of chopped parsley
extra virgin olive oil
balsamic vinegar
freshly cracked pepper
sea salt

Method

Place the shank into a pot of cold water so that it is well covered. Add the carrots, onion, celery and leek. Simmer for at least an hour or until the shank is tender. When it is done, take the shank out of the broth and allow to cool. Strain the broth, allow to cool and keep in the refrigerator as a soup base.

Once cooled the shank is thinly sliced. Peel and slice the shallots. Put veal and shallots together in a salad bowl, add some olive oil and toss. Add a few drops of the balsamic vinegar and season with salt and pepper. Add the parsley, toss once again and serve as part of the antipasto.

BARBECUED DUCK BREAST

Choose a duck with good breast meat. Trim the duck leaving the two breasts on the bone. Salt the skin on the breast and place in a roasting pan in a high oven till the skin is golden.

Place the breast skin down on the grill to crisp, then take breast meat off the bone and slice. The meat should still be pink. Sprinkle with balsamic vinegar and serve on some *rucola*.

DUCK-LEG PATTIES

Ingredients
the meat from 4 duck legs
2 slices day-old white of the bread, soaked in milk
4 tablespoons finely sliced leek
1 whole egg
salt and pepper
olive oil

Method
Work the meat and bread in the food processor. Mix with the leek and egg. Season, form into little patties and fry in olive oil till golden. Serve when cooled with a little fresh tomato sauce (page 26).

CAPSICUM AND EGGPLANT ROTOLO

Rotolo means 'roll'. Here we are making a pasta roll using capsicum and eggplant.

The tomato sauce
Make the sauce first, even a day or two ahead. Chop very finely one onion, one carrot, a stick of celery and garlic to taste. Lightly fry the vegetables in 5 tablespoons of extra virgin olive oil until tender. Add 1 kg of fresh, ripe tomatoes, pureed, some basil and oregano leaves, and simmer gently for 30–40 minutes. Season to taste.

The filling
Roast, peel and deseed two red and two yellow, fleshy capsicum. Cut top to bottom lengths of 3–4 cm width. Thinly slice one medium eggplant and fry lightly in olive oil. Separate about 20 basil leaves from their stalks.

The pasta

Make the pasta using the basic recipe (page 30). Add cuttlefish ink to half (when adding the eggs to the flour) and leave the other half white. After rolling the pasta through your pasta machine, cut a black sheet and a white sheet, each the width of the rollers of the machine and a total of 30–35 cm in length. Cook each sheet carefully in a large pot of salted boiling water till *al dente*, transfer each quickly to a bowl of cold water to stop it cooking, then place each sheet flat on some damp tea towels ready for assembling.

Assembly

Spread some tomato sauce evenly over the black pasta sheet. Lay a section of red capsicum, then eggplant, then yellow capsicum, repeating this sequence for two-thirds the length of the sheet. Leave the final third for sealing. Scatter the basil leaves over the capsicum and the eggplant. Now cover the lot with the white pasta sheet and roll carefully as tightly as you can. Rest in the refrigerator for about an hour then serve as slices on the antipasto with some of the left-over tomato sauce.

ROAST POLENTA WITH PARMESAN AND PROSCIUTTO

Ingredients

leftover polenta cut into rectangles 2 cm wide, 5 cm long and 1 cm thick
allow 1 piece thinly shaved parmesan to fit on the polenta
allow 1 slice prosciutto per piece of polenta

Method

Place the parmesan on the polenta and wrap the prosciutto around the lot. Place in a preheated 150°C oven for 10 minutes. Serve as part of the antipasto.

SEASONAL BUYING

In Australia, you can buy just about everything just about always. But not only is a lot of produce especially good in its season — it's considerably cheaper.

Herbs are for the most part perennial, apart from sage (summer/autumn), French tarragon (summer/early autumn), basil (best in summer) and chervil (best any time but summer).

Lettuces are good all year, except for cos and radicchio which need the cold weather to develop the hearts (the part that is eaten).

Remember that Australian seasons are extended because of the size of the country, with winter season fruit and vegetables moving south through the year, and summer produce moving north, making regional choices all the more important. For example, when buying asparagus in March, make sure it's from Queensland and not the last of the South Australian. A good greengrocer will know, and advise you.

Of course, not everything is seasonal. But an attempt to develop the habit of eating — and gorging — seasonally has the additional benefit of keeping us in touch, in an increasingly enclosed, air-conditioned world, with the natural rhythm of the seasons, the rhythms by which we all used to conduct our lives.

A list of the seasonal fruits and vegetables precedes each group of menus in this book, starting with this one for winter. It's thorough, without being exhaustive, and should prove a reasonably good guide for the seasonally minded.

June to August

Vegetables

Globe artichokes (the first are the best)
Jerusalem artichokes
Fennel
Snow peas
Witlof
Sweet potatoes: better*
Leeks: better*
Savoy cabbages: better*

Chinese cabbages: better*
Peas: better*
Radicchio: better*
Cauliflower
Brussels sprouts
Fennel
Broccoli
Cabbage

Fruit

Winter oranges, navels
Lemons
Mandarins
Grapefruit
Apples

Avocadoes
Tamarillos
Mangosteens
Custard apples

EVEN THOUGH OUR WINTERS here are mild, there's still an emotional need for warm, nourishing winter foods. For a northern Italian, that means polenta. And for this northern Italian that means refried, rebaked or reroast polenta — a slab of cooked polenta with a piece of aged parmesan in the middle, roasted until the cheese melts, or wrapped with prosciutto and fried. This smells like winter.

Winter is also about the more subtle tastes: pumpkins, for example. In winter we make *tortelli di zucca*, pasta stuffed with pumpkin and served with burnt butter and parmesan. In a way this dish exemplifies the turnaround in seasons: for us it's a Christmas dish and mounds of it are eaten at *la vigilia*, Christmas Eve.

But there are compensations. In Sydney, the seafood is wonderful now: king prawns from Yamba; baby crays from Tasmania. In The Restaurant Manfredi we'll often do a seafood

---

* Even though these vegetables are available all year round, they are at their best now.

ragu, based on a shellfish stock with mussels, crabs, clams, cuttlefish and pieces of cold-water fish, like grouper, served with *pasta stracci*, little rags of pasta; or sardines from Western Australia, stuffed with roast garlic puree, baked and served on a bed of winter greens.

It's time for *passati*, purees of root vegetables, turnip or jerusalem artichokes, simmered in water, veal or chicken stock, then strained and passed through the mouli, mixed with a little olive oil and served with crusty bread.

Then there are winter fruit, like oranges, and quince cooked slowly in a little wine and served with *gelati* spiced with cinnamon quills and star anise.

Winter is short days and long, slow cooking; osso buco is a seasonal favourite, or veal rib and lentil soup, with the leafy tops of turnips thrown in at the last minute before serving.

Artichokes are in season now, young and tender. If I can get them young enough I will do an artichoke salad that I first had in Milan, thinly sliced and dressed with olive oil and a little balsamic vinegar.

Because winters are mild, every now and then we'll snap back into summer to remind ourselves that it's not that far away; we'll do pan fried neck chops with peperonata (page 129), braised red capsicum, garlic, onions, basil and tomato.

And to end a meal, the marvellous and traditional northern Italian combination of dessert wine and spiced, nutty biscuit, **Vin Santo** and *biscotti*.

WINTER RECIPES

Mushrooms braised in white wine
Braised borlotti beans in white wine
Braised porcini mushrooms and polenta
Mussel and saffron broth with fresh garlic
Ox tongue with baby beetroot, turnips and capers
Braised pieces of cod with borlotti beans and polenta
Veal shank broth with winter vegetables
Roast veal fillet with dried tomatoes and sage
Anchovy, roast garlic and dried olive crostini
Warm salad of schnapper, beans and radicchio
Stir fried bok choy with garlic
Roast beef fillet with herbs
Jervis Bay oyster and sweet onion tart
Hare salmi with summer truffles and polenta
Yabbies and snow pea shoots in a light shellfish broth
Mussel and saffron risotto
Roast pork 'momboli' with red wine and sage sauce
Veal shank and borlotti bean soup
Roast white rabbit with radicchio and balsamic vinegar
Bitter chocolate tart with espresso gelato
Lattughe (fried pastries)
Panforte
Vanilla and butterscotch semifreddo
Chocolate buttermilk cake
Frozen pistachio nougatine

WINTER — JUNE TO AUGUST

WINTER MENU

Veal shank and borlotti bean soup
Braised porcini mushrooms and polenta
Roast veal fillet with dried tomatoes and sage
Bitter chocolate tart with espresso gelato

Mussel and saffron broth with fresh garlic
Mushrooms braised in white wine
Braised pieces of cod with borlotti beans and polenta
Vanilla and butterscotch semifreddo

Mussel and saffron risotto
Stir fried bok choy with garlic
Roast beef fillet with herbs
Frozen pistachio nougatine

Anchovy, roast garlic and dried olive crostini
Warm salad of schnapper, beans and radicchio
Jervis Bay oyster and sweet onion tart
Chocolate buttermilk cake

Veal shank broth with winter vegetables
Braised borlotti beans in white wine
Roast white rabbit with radicchio and balsamic vinegar
Lattughe — Fried pastries and panforte with coffee

MUSHROOMS BRAISED IN WHITE WINE

One of the best ways to show the different flavours, textures and colours of mushrooms is to combine several varieties as in this preparation.

SERVES 6 AS A FIRST COURSE

Ingredients

1/4 cup extra virgin olive oil
1 large onion, cut into small chunks
3 cloves garlic, crushed
1 kg assorted fresh mushrooms — buttons, field mushrooms, oyster (leave whole), shiitake, etc.(sliced)
1/3 cup dry white wine
1 handful parsley, chopped fine
salt and pepper
1 knob butter (optional)

Method

Heat oil in a pot and add onions, garlic and mushrooms. Stir continually for 1½–2 minutes. Add wine, bring to the boil then turn down to a simmer. Add the parsley and simmer for 8–10 minutes. Season and add butter if you like.

Serve on toast, with steak or roast quails or scrambled eggs.

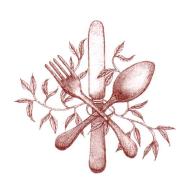

WINTER — JUNE TO AUGUST

BRAISED BORLOTTI BEANS IN WHITE WINE

SERVES 8 AS A FIRST COURSE

Ingredients

5 tablespoons extra virgin olive oil

2 carrots, peeled and chopped into half rounds

1 stick celery, sliced into 1/2-cm sections

1 medium onion, chopped

3 medium, ripe tomatoes, peeled and chopped

1 cup dry white wine

1 kg borlotti beans (shelled, this yields about 500 g)

3 cloves garlic, minced

large handful parsley, chopped fine

salt and pepper

Method

Put the olive oil in a saucepan, add the carrots, celery and onion and fry gently till the vegetables have softened. Add the tomatoes and the wine, bring to the boil, then add the borlotti. Simmer for 10 minutes then add the garlic and parsley. Simmer until the beans are cooked then season and serve hot with crusty bread or polenta.

BRAISED PORCINI MUSHROOMS AND POLENTA

Porcini is the Italian name for *Boletus edulus*, a mushroom with a deep, intense odour and flavour that intensifies with drying. Be careful when buying these: if they don't have that intense odour, they aren't porcini.

SERVES 6 AS A FIRST COURSE

Ingredients

50 g dried *porcini* mushrooms

500 g button mushrooms

1 large onion, roughly chopped

1 leek, sliced

4 cloves garlic, minced

olive oil

half cup dry white wine

large handful parsley, chopped

salt and pepper

Method

Soften the *porcini* by soaking them in cold water. Chop the button mushrooms into bite-size pieces.

Place the onion, leek and garlic in a pot with some olive oil and fry gently. Add all the mushrooms and stir continuously at high heat until they soften.

Add the wine and bring to the boil. Simmer for about 15 minutes then add the parsley and season.

Serve with polenta and a little grated parmesan.

MUSSEL AND SAFFRON BROTH WITH FRESH GARLIC

SERVES 4

Ingredients

2 kg mussels, washed and beard removed

1 cup dry white wine

1 leek, sliced

2–3 fresh garlic bulbs

2 ripe tomatoes, roughly chopped

pinch of saffron threads

salt and pepper

4 tablespoons extra virgin olive oil

WINTER — JUNE TO AUGUST

Method

In a large pot put the mussels, wine, garlic, tomatoes, leek and half the saffron threads. Place on high heat and cover with lid. Shake the pot every now and then until the mussels open. Drain, reserving the broth. Take the mussels out of their shells and distribute evenly among the soup plates.

Add the remaining saffron threads to the broth, put back into the pot, return to the boil and then season. Ladle some of the broth into the bowls containing the mussels and finish by adding one tablespoon of olive oil to each.

OX TONGUE WITH BABY BEETROOT, TURNIPS AND CAPERS

SERVES 4–6 AS A MAIN COURSE

Cooking the tongue

Ingredients

2 or 3 ox tongues, according to size

1 carrot, 1 onion, a stick of celery, cut into rough chunks

1/2 cup vinegar

Method

Place the tongues, vegetables and vinegar in a pot that is large enough to hold everything comfortably. Cover with cold water and bring to the boil. Turn the heat down to a simmer and cover the pot with a tight-fitting lid.

The tongue will take anything from 45 minutes upwards to cook. The way to tell if it is ready is to prod the thick end of the tongue with a sharp knife. If the meat is done it will be tender but still firm. The tough outer skin of the tongue should peel easily when cooked.

Keep the peeled tongues in their cooking liquid in a bowl. As long as they are completely covered by the liquid they will keep a long time in the refrigerator.

Cooking beetroot and turnips

Trim the leafy part of 3 medium-sized beetroots and 3 medium-sized turnips, and place them in separate saucepans, covered with water. Add ¼ cup vinegar, cover and simmer both until they are *al dente*. Once cooked, these can be stored in their liquid until needed.

Assembling the dish

about 2 tablespoons capers
4 tablespoons balsamic vinegar
salt and cracked pepper

Place 3 cups of the tongue liquid and 1 cup of the beetroot liquid in a pot. Add the tongues, capers, vinegar and cracked pepper and heat gently. When the tongues are steaming hot, add the beetroot and the turnips for about 5 minutes.

To serve, slice the tongues and place on plates with some juice and some beetroots and turnips. Season with salt to taste. Accompany the tongue with a leaf salad or steaming vegetables dressed with good olive oil.

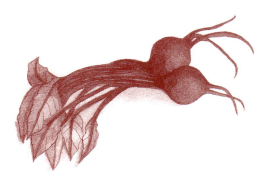

BRAISED PIECES OF COD WITH BORLOTTI BEANS AND POLENTA

SERVES 6–8 AS A MAIN COURSE

Ingredients

5 tablespoons extra virgin olive oil

2 carrots, peeled and chopped into half rounds

1 stick celery, sliced into 1/2-cm sections

1 medium onion, chopped

3 medium, ripe tomatoes, peeled and chopped

1 cup dry white wine

1 kg borlotti beans (shelled, this yields about 500 g)

3 cloves garlic, minced

large handful parsley, chopped fine

a sprig each of basil and thyme

salt and pepper

2–3 pieces cod (blue eye or bar cod) for each person

polenta (page 31)

Method

Put the olive oil in a saucepan, add the carrots, celery and onion and fry gently till the vegetables have softened. Add the tomatoes and the wine, bring to the boil then add the borlotti. Simmer for 10 minutes then add the garlic, parsley, basil and thyme. Simmer until the beans are cooked, then season.

Place the cooked beans in a wide sauté pan and (on top of the beans) arrange the pieces of cod evenly so that they are not over-lapping and they are covered by the liquid. Simmer gently for 3–5 minutes until they are done. Serve on top of some steaming polenta immediately.

VEAL SHANK BROTH WITH WINTER VEGETABLES

SERVES 8–10

Ingredients

1 veal shank, trimmed of excess fat and skin
2 carrots, cut into chunks
1 onion, cut into small wedges
3 sticks celery, cut into 2-cm lengths
2 leeks, cleaned and trimmed
some shallots, peeled and kept whole
3 medium potatoes, peeled and cut into pieces
a few brussels sprouts, trimmed and halved
6 cloves garlic, peeled and kept whole
1/4 of a small Savoy cabbage, sliced into strips
2 medium, ripe tomatoes, roughly chopped
a large handful of chopped parsley
extra virgin olive oil
freshly grated parmesan cheese
freshly cracked pepper
sea salt

Method

Place the shank into a pot of cold water so that it is well covered. Simmer for about 40 minutes then add the vegetables. Simmer for another 20–30 minutes. When the shank is tender, turn off the heat, take it out of the soup and cut it into small pieces. Return these pieces to the soup and add the chopped parsley. Season and serve with some crusty bread and freshly grated parmesan cheese. Add a tablespoon of olive oil to each bowl.

ROAST VEAL FILLET WITH DRIED TOMATOES AND SAGE

SERVES 4 AS A MAIN COURSE

Ingredients

1 veal fillet weighing 750–850 g, trimmed

150 g dried tomatoes (make sure they're soft, not stiff)

1 bunch sage

4 tablespoons olive oil

100 g pork net (caul fat)

salt and pepper

Method

Make sure that the veal fillet is trimmed of all skin and fat. Cut 3–4 cm off the thin end of the fillet so that it is reasonably uniform. With a sharp knife start to open out the fillet from top to bottom like a scroll. It should open out to about four times its width. Lay the dried tomatoes evenly along a line the length of the fillet about 3 cm from one end. Season the entire surface of the flattened fillet and scatter the sage leaves evenly over the area. Roll the fillet as tightly as you can so that it resembles approximately its original shape. Spread out the caul net and place the veal fillet on it, wrapping the meat securely.

Place the entire parcel in a baking dish, brush with olive oil and bake in a preheated oven at 220°C for 15–20 minutes. Rest for a further 20 minutes then slice and serve with the baking juices.

ANCHOVY, ROAST GARLIC AND DRIED OLIVE CROSTINI

SERVES 6–8 AS A SNACK

To make crostini

Slice a *focaccia* into 2 cm x 4 cm pieces, at about $1/4$ cm in thickness. Brush some good olive oil on to both sides of each piece, place on a baking tray and heat in a warm oven (60°C) until they are crisp. Allow to cool. These *crostini* can now be stored in an airtight container until they are needed.

Anchovy and roast garlic paste

Ingredients

6 bulbs garlic
150–200 g anchovy fillets, drained of oil
1/4 cup extra virgin olive oil
salt and pepper to taste

Method

Preheat the oven to 150°C. Place the garlic bulbs on a baking tray and roast in the oven until they are soft and creamy inside. This should take 20–30 minutes. Allow to cool, then slice the bulbs in half, across the cloves, and squeeze the garlic out like toothpaste into the bowl of a food processor. Add the anchovies and olive oil and blend until smooth. Add the salt and pepper.

Now it is ready to use. Spread on the crostini with some chopped black olives.

WARM SALAD OF SCHNAPPER, BEANS AND RADICCHIO

SERVES 6 AS A MAIN COURSE

Ingredients

one 3-kg schnapper, filleted and boned, with the skin left on
6 tablespoons olive oil for frying
500 g small green beans, cooked in boiling salted water briefly
  (so that they are still *al dente*) and allowed to cool
2 radicchio hearts, washed and sliced into thick strips lengthways
6 tablespoons roast garlic and anchovy dressing (page 72)
salt and pepper to taste

Method

Preheat the oven to 250°C. Cut the fish into six roughly even pieces, pulling out any bones with a pair of tweezers. Put the olive oil evenly into two skillets and heat until it just *starts* to smoke. Sprinkle some salt on the skin side of each of the pieces of schnapper and place them gently, skin side down, in the hot oil. Fry for about 30 second then turn them.

Now place the skillets, assuming they are ovenproof, in the oven for about 7 minutes. If the skillets are not ovenproof, transfer the fish to a baking dish and bake for 7–10 minutes.

Meanwhile, place the beans and radicchio in a large mixing bowl and toss with the anchovy and garlic dressing, adding pepper and salt if necessary. Distribute among the six plates and place a piece of fish on each. Serve immediately.

STIR FRIED BOK CHOY WITH GARLIC

Wandering around Chinatown (which is very close to The Restaurant Manfredi and getting closer as it expands) I notice all these exotic Asian vegetables. What do I do? I take them back to the kitchen and teach them Italian. This is one of those dishes.

SERVES 6 AS AN ACCOMPANIMENT TO ROAST BEEF FILLET WITH HERBS (BELOW).

Ingredients

6 tablespoons olive oil
2 bunches small bok choy, washed and the leaves separated
6 cloves garlic, minced
1/4 cup chicken stock or light veal stock
salt and pepper to taste

Method

Heat the olive oil in a large skillet or wok until it is just smoking. Throw in the bok choy and garlic and stir well for 2–3 minutes. It should wilt fairly quickly within that time. Now add the chicken or veal stock and season with the salt and pepper. Serve immediately.

ROAST BEEF FILLET WITH HERBS

SERVES 6 AS A MAIN MEAL

Ingredients

a mixture of fresh herbs with their branches and stems removed. This may contain parsley, basil, oregano, rosemary, dill, sage, thyme and chives.
1.2 kg beef tenderloin, trimmed of all fat and skin
3 tablespoons olive oil
salt and pepper

Method

Preheat the oven to a temperature of 250°C. Chop the herbs together with a large knife or *mezzaluna* until they are quite fine. Rub the beef fillet all over with the olive oil. Season with salt and pepper. Roll the fillet in the mixture of herbs so that it is well coated. Place the fillet in a baking dish and roast for 20 minutes.

Remove from the oven and rest for about 20 minutes in a warm place. Slice and serve with the stir fried bok choy. The beef should be quite rare.

JERVIS BAY OYSTER AND SWEET ONION TART

The Jervis Bay oysters grow on the south coast of New South Wales and are similar to the French Belon oysters. They are particularly good when pan fried and served on a salad or as in this recipe on a tart.

SERVES 6–8 AS A FIRST COURSE

The Pastry

Ingredients

250 g flour
125 g butter
60 g parmesan, grated
1 whole egg

Method

Bring all the ingredients together in the food processor with a few short bursts. Shape into a log, cover with cling wrap and refrigerate until needed.

The tarts

Ingredients

pastry dough (as on p.75)
4 egg yolks
50 g grated parmesan
500 ml cream
salt and pepper to taste
2 sweet onions, thinly sliced
olive oil
6 oysters per tart, per person
some chopped fennel tops

Method

Cut off sections of dough and press into tart cases. Rest in the refrigerator. Preheat the oven to 180°C. Bake the cases until they are lightly golden.

Mix the egg yolks, parmesan and cream together. Season, then rest.

Lightly fry the onions in a little olive oil until they are soft. Place some onion in each tart shell, then pour some of the egg yolk mixture over this, to about two-thirds full. Put the tarts back in the oven and bake until they are set.

To finish off, lightly fry the oysters in a little olive oil and place them on top of the tarts, then garnish with chopped fennel tops. Serve with young *rucola* leaves.

HARE SALMI WITH SUMMER TRUFFLES AND POLENTA

Summer truffles are not as highly regarded as winter truffles. They are still black, but lighter on the inside and not as intensely flavoured. They're available in Sydney from McDonald and Johnson, in Melbourne from Enoteca Sileno. And, of course, in Australia, we get them in winter. The hare you will get from a specialty game butcher, and it's one of the few true game meats available commercially in Australia.

SERVES 8 AS A MAIN COURSE

Ingredients

2 hares — legs, shoulders, fillets and livers removed
2 carrots, peeled and chopped into thick rounds
3 sticks celery, cut into pieces as thick as the carrots
2 onions, peeled and cut into chunks
4 ripe tomatoes, peeled, seeded and chopped
8–10 cloves garlic, chopped, not minced
2 sticks cinnamon, broken up
12 whole cloves
rind of 1 lemon
dry red wine (enough to cover the hare and vegetables)
1 summer truffle, cut in thin slices
olive oil
salt and pepper

Method

Take the hare legs and shoulders and place them in a tub with the vegetables, tomatoes, garlic, cinnamon, cloves and lemon rind. Cover with the red wine and allow to sit in the refrigerator and marinate overnight.

The next day separate the liquid from the hare and the vegetables and reserve it. In a heavy bottom casserole pot, sweat the hare and vegetables in about $1/4$ cup olive oil for about 10 minutes, continually stirring with a wooden spoon. Add the reserved wine and truffle and simmer for about $1 1/2$ hours.

Take the four hare fillets and sear them on a high heat in some olive oil in a frying pan. Rest them for about 20 minutes in a warm place, then slice thinly and serve with some of the vegetables and the sauce. Make sure these have been seasoned well before serving. Serve with steaming polenta.

YABBIES AND SNOW PEA SHOOTS IN A LIGHT SHELLFISH BROTH

SERVES 8–10

Ingredients

2 kg freshwater crayfish (yabbies)
4 tablespoons cooking salt
1 leek, cleaned and roughly chopped
1 carrot, cut into 1-cm rounds
1 stick celery, cut into 1-cm pieces
1 onion, peeled and halved
2 ripe tomatoes, roughly chopped
1 handful snow pea shoots
salt and pepper
10 teaspoons extra virgin olive oil

Method

Bring enough water to the boil so that the crayfish fit comfortably in the pot, submerged. Into the boiling water put the salt and the crayfish and cook until the water comes back to the boil. Drain the crayfish and throw some ice on them to refresh. Remove the tail meat and set it aside, keeping the shells and the heads.

Place the tails and shells in a large pot of fresh, cold water, adding the vegetables (not the snow peas). Simmer for at least 2 hours but don't boil. Strain the broth and season.

To serve, put crayfish meat and tails, and snow pea shoots and one teaspoon of extra virgin olive oil in each plate. Reheat the broth and pour over.

MUSSEL AND SAFFRON RISOTTO

SERVES 6 AS A MAIN COURSE

Ingredients

2 litres fish and shellfish stock (page 24)
100 ml extra virgin olive oil
1 onion, finely chopped
2 cloves garlic, minced
2 cups Arborio rice
20 strands saffron
handful grated parmesan (optional)
2 kg mussels, steamed, shelled and the liquid kept
salt and pepper

Method

Heat the stock and keep it to hand, simmering. In a pot heat the olive oil and gently fry the onion and garlic until they become transparent. Add the rice and continue to fry gently for 2 minutes. Add the saffron threads, then ladle some of the simmering broth into the rice. As it is absorbed, continue to add some broth until the risotto is cooked but still *al dente*. Fold in the parmesan and add the mussels. Season and rest for 5 minutes, then serve.

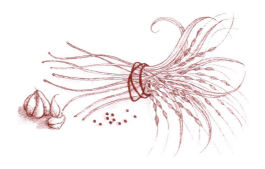

ROAST PORK MOMBOLI WITH RED WINE AND SAGE SAUCE

SERVES 4 AS MAIN COURSE

Ingredients

2 pork fillets, butterflied open with a knife
4 slices prosciutto
sage and rosemary
salt and pepper to taste
1/2 cup dry red wine
1 tablespoon butter

Method

Place the open pork fillets in front of you and cover with the prosciutto. Sprinkle evenly with sage and rosemary leaves. Season, then roll like a long sausage, fixing the roll with toothpicks. Place in a small baking dish, add the wine and butter and some more sage leaves and roast in a preheated oven for 15–20 minutes. Remove the *momboli*, then return the sauce to the oven to reduce. Slice the pork, and serve with the sauce and steamed green vegetables.

Momboli is a dialect word which is derived from the Italian *lombi*, meaning the loin meat of pork.

VEAL SHANK AND BORLOTTI BEAN SOUP

SERVES AT LEAST 10–12

Ingredients

2 veal shanks

3 carrots, peeled and cut into chunks

3 sticks celery, cut into chunks

3 medium potatoes, peeled and cut into 6–8 pieces

2 large onions, peeled and cut into chunks

1 garlic bulb, peeled and cloves left whole

large handful continental parsley, taken off the stem

6 ripe tomatoes, roughly chopped

750 g borlotti beans, out of pods

100 g freshly grated parmesan

salt and pepper to taste

Method

Place the shanks in a large pot of cold, fresh water and bring to the boil. Simmer for 45 minutes, then add all the vegetables and parsley and simmer for a further 30–45 minutes until the vegetables are cooked.

Take out the veal shank with a pair of tongs and take all the tender meat off the bone, cutting it into smaller manageable pieces.

Return this meat to the soup, season with salt and pepper and serve with grated parmesan and crusty bread. The left-over soup will keep well and in fact get better over 2–3 days.

ROAST WHITE RABBIT WITH RADICCHIO AND BALSAMIC VINEGAR

These aren't the wild rabbits, which are smaller and gamier in flavour, but domesticated rabbits, which are larger and more tender. They're usually available from specialty game butchers.

SERVES 8

Ingredients

3 tablespoons olive oil
2 full heads radicchio, roughly chopped
1 large onion, thinly sliced
2 cloves garlic, crushed
2 white rabbits, each weighing about 1 kg
balsamic vinegar
50 g butter
salt and pepper
1 cup dry white wine

Method

Heat oven to 200°C.

Into a roasting dish large enough to take the two rabbits comfortably, pour the olive oil and spread the radicchio, onions and garlic evenly. Place the rabbits on top and spray them with the vinegar. Distribute the butter in knobs all round the dish, with some on the rabbits. Season well and place in the oven.

After 10 minutes pour the wine over the rabbits, basting them. Roast until the rabbits are done. This should take another 20–30 minutes, according to their size.

Serve with a salad of mixed greens.

BITTER CHOCOLATE TART WITH ESPRESSO GELATO

MAKES ONE 20-CM TART TO SERVE 8

Pastry

Ingredients

175 g plain flour
1/4 teaspoon baking powder
pinch salt
65 g caster sugar
125 g chilled butter
1 egg yolk

Method

Mix together the flour, baking powder, salt and sugar. Work in the butter and egg quickly. Rest in refrigerator for at least 1 hour. Roll out onto a 20-cm pie tin and rest again for 1/2 hour.

Filling

Ingredients

150 g caster sugar
85 g softened butter
zest of 1/2 an orange, grated
2 eggs, beaten
1 tablespoon plain flour
200 g roasted hazelnuts, skinned and chopped
90 g dark chocolate, grated
2 tablespoons orange liqueur (preferably Aurum)

Method

Cream the sugar and butter and add the zest. Mix in the eggs, flour, hazelnuts, chocolate and liqueur. Pour the filling into the pie shell and bake for 30 minutes at 180°C.

Gelato

Ingredients

185 g sugar

8 egg yolks

1 litre cream

10 very short cups espresso coffee

1 teaspoon finely ground coffee beans

Method

Beat sugar and egg yolks together until they are pale.

Heat the cream almost to the boil. Don't boil. Whisk in the egg-sugar mixture. Place on a low heat and stir continuously with wooden spoon until it thickens and coats the spoon. Add the coffee and the ground beans, then cool completely before churning.

LATTUGHE (FRIED PASTRIES)

These delicious little morsels have a different name in just about every region of Italy: *crostoli*, *cenci*, *chiacchere*, etc. This version, from Lombardy, is particularly light.

MAKES 40 LATTUGHE

Ingredients

5 eggs, separated
40 g butter
50 g sugar
1 nip grappa
grated rind of 1 lemon
juice of 1 lemon
1 tablespoon baking powder
750 g plain flour
duck fat or goose fat or, as a last resort, olive oil
icing sugar

Method

Beat the egg yolks, sugar and butter together. Add the grappa, lemon juice and rind, mixing. Whisk the egg whites to soft peaks then mix in.

Add the flour and baking powder. Work to a dough. Roll out as you would pasta and cut into rectangles about 5 cm x 3 cm.

Place the duck fat into a frying pan and fry the pastries, turning them once in the pan. They should be golden brown. Dust them with icing sugar while they are warm.

PANFORTE

Panforte means 'strong bread' and is a specialty of Siena in Tuscany. There are hundreds of versions of *panforte*. This particular one is neither as hard nor as sweet as many of the others you may have tried.

MAKES ONE TRAY 38 CM X 26 CM

Ingredients

250 g blanched almonds, roasted
250 g hazelnuts, roasted
750 g various dried fruits (raisins, peel, prunes, etc)
1 tablespoon cinnamon
1 tablespoon mixed spice
250 g plain flour
310 g sugar
310 g honey
rice paper sheets

Method

Line a 38 cm x 26 cm sponge or jelly roll tray with rice paper.

Mix together the nuts, dried fruits, spice and flour. Heat the sugar and honey together until they reach the soft ball stage (118°C). Add this to the nut and fruit mixture and spoon into the tray. Don't worry if the mixture is not evenly spread out as it will settle down in cooking. Cover the top of the mixture with rice paper and bake for 20 minutes at 170°C.

Allow to cool, then cut into small pieces.

VANILLA AND BUTTERSCOTCH SEMIFREDDO

Caramelised sticks

Roll a piece of puff pastry into a rectangle 10–12 cm wide. Sprinkle sugar onto the pastry and roll it in. Now cut 1–1$\frac{1}{2}$ cm sticks, twisting each 3 or 4 times. Rest in the refrigerator on baking trays for $\frac{1}{2}$ hour. Bake at 220°C until the sugar begins to caramelise then turn the sticks and finish baking them. Cool and store in an airtight container.

Vanilla bean gelato

1 litre single cream
2 vanilla beans
200 g caster sugar
8 egg yolks

Prepare the ingredients as per *crema inglese* (page 38), cool then churn.

Butterscotch sauce

800 g brown sugar
500 ml single cream
400 g unsalted butter

Heat all ingredients in a saucepan and whisk until the butter is entirely incorporated.

Assembly

On each plate place two of the pastry sticks, balancing a wedge of vanilla gelato on top. Repeat another layer then spoon some hot butterscotch sauce over the top and serve.

CHOCOLATE BUTTERMILK CAKE

MAKES 1 CAKE TO SERVE 12–15

Ingredients

2 cups plain flour, sifted
80 g cocoa
1 1/2 teaspoons bicarbonate of soda
1/2 teaspoon baking powder
375 g caster sugar
1 1/2 cups buttermilk
1 teaspoon vanilla essence
3 eggs
125 g melted butter
200 g dark chocolate, melted
300 g dark chocolate, for the icing
400 ml condensed milk, for the icing

Method

Mix together the five dry ingredients. Add the buttermilk, vanilla and eggs to the dry mixture and beat well until it has formed a batter. Add the melted butter and melted chocolate and mix in.

Grease and line a 20 cm x 30 cm cake tin and pour in the cake mixture. Place in a preheated 160°C oven. Bake for 30 minutes then check to see if it is set. It should take 30–40 minutes and should be baked till just set.

Take from the oven and leave in the tin to cool for 20 minutes. Turn out onto a cake rack to cool completely.

Melt the chocolate with the condensed milk in a small saucepan over low heat and use this to ice the cake. Don't refrigerate. Serve with almond custard and ginger *biscotti* (recipes opposite).

Almond custard

Ingredients

2 vanilla beans, split and scraped
200 g almond meal
750 ml milk
9 egg yolks
180 g caster sugar
4 leaves gelatine
10 ml almond essence
375 ml cream

Method

Place the vanilla beans, the almond meal and the milk in a saucepan and bring to the boil. Cream the egg yolks and the sugar together and strain the hot milk onto this, whisking well. Soak the gelatine leaves in a little water.

Bring the mixture back to a medium heat and stir until the custard coats the back of the spoon. Transfer then to a cool bowl, add the gelatine and the almond essence and mix thoroughly until the gelatine has completely dissolved. Place in the refrigerator to cool.

Meanwhile whip the cream and fold into the custard when completely cool. Return to refrigerator until needed.

Ginger biscotti

MAKES ABOUT 150

Ingredients

250 g butter
250 g sugar
125 g brown sugar
125 g honey
3 egg whites
550 g flour
2 teaspoons baking powder
400 g finely diced glacé ginger

Method

Cream the butter, sugars and honey together, then mix in the egg whites one at a time. Add the flour and the baking powder, mixing well to form a dough. Work in the ginger then refrigerate to set the mixture.

Preheat the oven at 140°C. Roll the dough into small balls and set on a cookie tray, pressing each ball down with a wet fork. Bake for about 15 minutes until golden brown. Remove from the tray while they are still hot.

FROZEN PISTACHIO NOUGATINE

Nougatines traditionally contain praline cream. Nougatine cakes are layered with sponge and nougatine cream.

MAKES 14 NOUGATINES

Custard

Ingredients

120 g sugar

3 egg yolks

200 ml single cream

1 vanilla bean, split and scraped

Method

Whisk the sugar and yolks together until they are pale and form a ribbon.* Heat the cream and the vanilla bean until almost at the boil, whisk into the egg mixture and return to a moderate heat, stirring continuously until the custard coats the back of the spoon. Transfer to a bowl and allow to cool.

---

* For explanation, see page 38.

Praline

Ingredients

150 g sugar

100 g hazelnuts, roasted, skinned and chopped fine

100 g almonds, roasted and chopped fine

100 g pistachios, roasted and cut into small chunks

Method

Bring the sugar to the boil and cook to a light caramel. Place the hazelnuts, almonds and pistachios in a tray and pour the caramel over them. Allow to cool, then pound the praline until it is fine.

PISTACHIO *BISCOTTI*

MAKES 50

Ingredients

2 cups sugar

4 eggs

4 cups flour

1 teaspoon baking powder

400 g pistachios, roasted and left whole

2 egg whites, lightly beaten

extra flour for working the dough

Method

In the food processor blend the sugar and eggs. Add the 4 cups of flour one at a time. Add the baking powder with the last cup of flour. Turn the dough out onto a well-floured surface and work in the pistachios. Knead the dough, adding more flour if necessary until it is firm.

Divide the dough in half, forming two logs. Flatten these so that they are about 3 cm high. Brush each log with the egg white, place on a greased baking tray and bake in a preheated oven at 140°C for 30 minutes.

Take from the oven, allow to sit for 10 minutes then, while still hot, slice into ½-cm biscuits. Place these on baking trays and return to the oven at 80°C for 10–15 minutes to dry. Allow to cool before serving.

Caramellised figs

Ingredients
allow 1 fig per person
caster sugar

Method
Cut the figs in half, top to bottom, and lay them down cut side up. Sprinkle gradually with caster sugar while applying the heat of a domestic blowtorch. When the sugar has turned a golden caramel colour the fig is ready. Repeat for all the figs.

Assembly

Ingredients
125 g sugar
60 g honey
30 g glucose syrup
50 ml water
6 egg whites
zest of 1 lemon
300 ml double cream

Method
Bring the sugar, honey, glucose syrup and water to the boil in a saucepan until it reaches the 'soft ball' stage. Whip the egg whites to form soft peaks. While still whisking, pour in the sugar syrup and keep whisking until the mixture has cooled.

Now fold in the custard, the praline, lemon zest and the double cream. Transfer the mixture to individual moulds and freeze.

To serve, unmould on the plate and accompany with the caramellised figs and pistachio *biscotti*.

September to November

Vegetables

Broad beans (young beans are the best)	Eggplant
Asparagus	Zucchini flowers
Snow peas	Fennel
Spring onions	Kununurra onions
Witlof	

Fruit

Mangoes start	Early apricots
End of the custard apples	Strawberries (best now)
Early peaches	Pawpaws (best now)
Pineapples (Queensland rough leaf are particularly sweet)	Early nectarines

SPRING STARTS WITH BROAD BEANS and asparagus, the baby broad beans almost causing mutiny in the kitchen. I like them double peeled, and it's such fiddly work but one of those things you must do in cooking, process being as important as product. Once peeled, we simmer them until tender and serve simply with mashed roast garlic.

Another fiddly food starting to come through is the zucchini flower: stuffed with a mixture of parmesan and bread crumbs, it is dipped in a very light batter and lightly fried in olive oil. And eggplants, purple and packed with flesh, are baked, peeled and mashed with garlic to spread over focaccia.

A new springtime treat for me are the Kununurra onions from the Ord River in Western Australia. They're a sweet onion, white with a yellow blush and a squashed oval shape. We do them in a tart with fennel and lightly fried Nambucca oysters dusted with parmesan; or cut in thick slabs, brushed with olive oil and dusted with paprika, cayenne pepper and fennel seeds, then lightly charred on the barbecue; or with sliced fennel bulb — another spring vegetable.

SPRING — SEPTEMBER TO NOVEMBER

And spring lamb. Although we now have lamb all year round, at this time of the year it's especially succulent.

Don't ask me why, but skate — the wings and fins of various rays and sharks — is good at this time, as are the wonderful Bruny Island mussels, which we use in a cannelloni with snow peas. Italian food has such wonderful forms — pizzas, lasagnes, risottos — within which we can play endless variations.

The first of the stone fruits come through now. We poach early peaches in *moscato* and serve them with a rich zabaglione, and bake nectarines into a layered sponge with Frangelico or Nocello liqueurs.

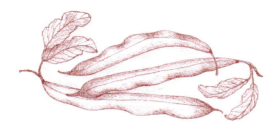

SPRING RECIPES

Salad of veal shank with beetroot and onion
Spanner crab and onion salad
Poached spring salmon with spring vegetables
Cannelloni with Bruny Island mussels and leeks
Tagliatelle with artichokes and parmesan
Taglierini with quail and pancetta
Crisp veal sweetbreads, roast eschallots and chilli salad
Grilled Coffin Bay scallops
with stir fried Chinese vegetables and garlic
Roast baby guinea fowl with herbs and fennel
Seared veal cutlet with sage
Lasagne of prawns, mussels, leek and eggplant
Frittata with leeks and basil
Beans, asparagus and fried prosciutto salad
Pasta stracci with brook trout and Sicilian caper salsa
Seared duck livers with fried prosciutto and parmesan potatoes
Mediterranean tuna
Stingray braised in tomato and fennel
Roast beef with asparagus and parmesan
Spring vegetable minestrone
Warm tripe salad with roast eschallots
Mulberry and almond pie
Peach and plum torta
Roast suckling leg of lamb with rosemary and roast potatoes
Rhubarb pudding
Venison cutlet with fresh tomato and basil sauce
Strawberry and mascarpone soffiati

SPRING — SEPTEMBER TO NOVEMBER

SPRING MENU

Salad of veal shank with beetroot and onion
Taglierini with quail and pancetta
Crisp veal sweetbreads, roast eschallots and chilli salad
Peach and plum torta

Spanner crab and onion salad
Tagliatelle with artichokes and parmesan
Poached spring salmon with spring vegetables
Strawberry and mascarpone soffiati

Spring vegetable minestrone
Warm tripe salad with roast eschallots
Roast baby guinea fowl with herbs and fennel
Mulberry and almond pie

Frittata with leeks and basil
Beans, asparagus and fried prosciutto salad
Pasta stracci with brook trout and Sicilian caper salsa
Rhubarb pudding

Grilled Coffin Bay scallops
with stir fried Chinese vegetables and garlic
Stringray braised in tomato and fennel
Cannelloni with Bruny Island mussels and leeks
Roast suckling leg of lamb with rosemary and roast potatoes

SALAD OF VEAL SHANK WITH BEETROOT AND ONION

SERVES 6 AS A FIRST COURSE

Ingredients

1 veal shank, trimmed of fat (about 500 g)
3 large fresh beetroot, unpeeled
3 large fresh onions, with skin on
6 tablespoons extra virgin olive oil
salad greens — rucola, endive, lamb's tongue
salt and pepper to taste

Method

Place the veal, beetroot and onions in a pot large enough to hold them comfortably. Cover with cold water. Bring to the boil and then immediately lower the heat, cover and simmer until the beetroot and onion are just cooked. This should take about 20 minutes. You can tell by piercing the beetroot and onions with a sharp knife.

At this point take the beet and the onions out and put aside to cool. The veal shank should simmer away for another 30–40 minutes. It is cooked when the meat feels tender when pierced with a fork. Take it out of the water and allow it to cool as well.

Peel the beetroot and onions and cut them into large wedges. Slice the veal shank into bite-size pieces. Add the salad leaves, dress all the ingredients with the olive oil, salt and pepper to taste, then serve.

SPANNER CRAB AND ONION SALAD

FOR 6 PEOPLE AS A FIRST COURSE

Ingredients

600 g fresh cooked spanner crab meat
$1/2$ Kunanurra onion or Spanish (red) onion, finely sliced
6 tablespoons extra virgin olive oil
2 cups full of shredded greens such as radicchio, rucola, etc.
salt and pepper to taste

Method

In a bowl mix the finely sliced onion, the crab meat and olive oil, and season. Toss so that all ingredients are mixed thoroughly and allow to sit for about 20 minutes. Arrange the shredded lettuce on the plates then place the crab mixture on top. Serve immediately.

POACHED SPRING SALMON WITH SPRING VEGETABLES

SERVES 8–10 AS A MAIN COURSE

Ingredients

one Tasmanian Atlantic salmon, filleted, skinned and boned
1/2 onion, roughly chopped
1 carrot, peeled and chopped into rounds
1 stick celery, chopped into rounds
2 cloves garlic, peeled and left whole
8 spring onions, peeled, trimmed and blanched
16–20 spears asparagus, cut into 2-cm lengths and blanched
1 cup fresh shelled peas, blanched
8–10 zucchini flowers, blanched
3 bunches tender rucola leaves
extra virgin olive oil for dressing
salt and pepper to taste

Method

In a poaching kettle or other appropriate container place the salmon together with the onion, celery, carrot and garlic. Cover with water and season. Turn on the heat and simmer until the fish is just cooked through. It should still be a creamy orange in the centre and this should take about 15 minutes. Take the salmon out of the poaching liquid and put aside to drain and cool.

Meanwhile, toss all the blanched spring vegetables and the *rucola* with the olive oil, season and distribute evenly onto plates. Tear the salmon into pieces, toss and dress with the remaining oil, and season. Place the salmon pieces on the plates with the spring vegetables and serve.

CANNELLONI WITH BRUNY ISLAND MUSSELS AND LEEKS

This is a classic Italian/Australian dish. Cannelloni — a form everyone knows, but expects to be filled with mince and sloppy cheese. Let's fill it instead with mussels from Bruny Island on the west coast of Tasmania, the sweetest, richest, fullest mussels you'll ever meet on a plate (you can use any fresh mussels, but the dish was inspired by these ones) and sweet leeks. Simple.

SERVES 6 AS A FIRST COURSE

Ingredients

olive oil
3 leeks, cleaned, washed and cut into thin rounds
pasta (page 00) rolled out into thin sheets
2 kg Bruny Island mussels, beards taken off, steamed open and shells discarded
2 cups fresh tomato and basil sauce (page 27)
1 cup grated mozzarella cheese
1/3 cup grated parmesan cheese
salt and pepper to taste

Method

Heat some olive oil in a pan and gently fry the leeks until they are soft.

Cut the sheets of pasta into 12 rectangles 6 cm by 10 cm. Cook immediately in plenty of fast boiling, salted water. Place the cooked sheets onto wet tea towels. Spoon some of the leeks onto each sheet, then 3–4 mussels. Now roll the cannelloni like a cigarette.

Spoon some of the tomato sauce onto the bottom of a baking dish. Arrange the cannelloni in the dish, distribute the tomato sauce on top, then the mozzarella and parmesan. Season and place in a preheated oven at 170°C for 15 minutes. Serve hot.

TAGLIATELLE WITH ARTICHOKES AND PARMESAN

Choosing and preparing artichokes

Choose artichokes as you would any other vegetable. They must be firm, with full heads and no blemishes. You'll need a sharp paring knife and a pot of cold water with the juice of one lemon squeezed into it.

Take the top of the artichoke clean off, then begin paring around the heart until you reach the tender inner leaves. Leave 3–5 cm of stalk at the base and trim away any leaves. As each artichoke is prepared, place it in the pot with the lemon water and cook until tender. Feel them with the point of a sharp knife.

SERVES 6 AS A FIRST COURSE

Ingredients

12 artichokes, prepared and cut into wedges

180 g butter

fresh tagliatelle

parmesan to taste; take shavings from the piece by using a vegetable peeler or sharp knife

freshly ground pepper

Method

Warm the bowls that will be used to serve the pasta. Distribute the butter and the artichoke pieces evenly. The butter should melt a little but not separate in the bowls.

Bring a pot of salted water to the boil and cook the tagliatelle until they are *al dente*. Drain well and distribute evenly among the waiting plates. Toss and serve with the parmesan and freshly ground pepper.

TAGLIERINI WITH QUAIL AND PANCETTA

SERVES 8 AS A FIRST COURSE

Ingredients

1/3 cup cup extra virgin olive oil
2 carrots, peeled and cut into small chunks
1 onion, peeled and cut into 1-cm chunks
2 sticks celery, cut into small chunks
4–5 garlic cloves, peeled and minced
2 cups chopped parsley
8–10 slices pancetta (unsmoked bacon), cut into strips
8 large quail, each cut into 4 pieces
1 cup dry white wine
2 cups veal stock
4 ripe tomatoes, roughly chopped
salt and pepper to taste
400 g freshly made taglierini (see basic pasta method, page 29)

Method

In a pot large enough to hold all the ingredients, heat the olive oil. Add the vegetables, parsley and pancetta and fry lightly for 5 minutes.

Now add the quail pieces and fry gently for another 5 minutes. Add the white wine and bring to the boil for 2–3 minutes. Add the veal stock and the tomatoes and simmer for 20 minutes until the quails are tender and the meat comes off the bone easily.

Take the quail out of the liquid, debone (rip small pieces of the cooked flesh from the carcass) and return the meat to the sauce. Season the sauce and serve on top of the freshly cooked taglierini with grated parmesan cheese.

CRISP VEAL SWEETBREADS, ROAST ESCHALLOTS AND CHILLI SALAD

Sweetbreads are the thymus glands of veal or lamb and not, as often thought, the testicles. In those countries where food is high in the list of cultural priorities, the insides of the animals are often more highly esteemed than the flesh.

SERVES 4

Ingredients

32 eschallots
olive oil
1 radicchio heart, leaves separated
1 small red onion, finely sliced
2–3 chillies, chopped fine
red wine vinegar
extra virgin olive oil
1 knob butter
500 g veal sweetbreads, blanched, peeled and sliced into bite-size pieces
salt and pepper to taste

Method

Preheat the oven to 160°C.

Place the eschallots on a roasting tray, sprinkle with olive oil and season. Roast until they are soft inside. Open them up by peeling away the layers of skin.

Place the radicchio, sliced onion, eschallots and chillies in a bowl, season and dress with a little vinegar and some extra virgin olive oil.

Now heat some olive oil and a little butter in a skillet and gently fry the sweetbreads until they are crisp on both sides. Season and serve on top of the salad.

GRILLED COFFIN BAY SCALLOPS WITH STIR FRIED CHINESE VEGETABLES AND GARLIC

SERVES 4 AS A FIRST COURSE

Ingredients

4 cloves garlic, minced

1/4 cup extra virgin olive oil

24 Coffin Bay scallops in their shells, cleaned and cut so that the scallop is only just attached to the shell

1 head each of the Chinese vegetables bok choy, gai lum, choy sum and een choy, washed and cut into large pieces

4 tablespoons chopped Italian parsley

Method

Mix a clove of the minced garlic in half the olive oil. Brush some of this oil onto each of the scallops then place them on an oven tray and set them under the grill or salamander for 3–5 minutes.

Meanwhile, heat the rest of the olive oil in a wok or large skillet. Add the Chinese vegetables and the rest of the garlic and stir fry at high heat until they are tender. Season and serve with the scallops. Sprinkle the parsley over the scallops and vegetables.

ROAST BABY GUINEA FOWL WITH HERBS AND FENNEL

SERVES 6 AS A MAIN COURSE

Ingredients

6 baby guinea fowl, each cut into two along the middle

1/3 cup extra virgin olive oil

a mixture of herbs (3–4 sprigs of each) — fennel leaves, sage, parsley, oregano, rosemary, thyme and basil, all chopped up together

freshly cracked pepper

sea salt

3 bulbs fennel, sliced top to bottom into thin wedges

Method

Spread the guinea fowl out in roasting trays and rub the skin of each with olive oil. Now roll each of the guinea fowl halves in the herbs so that the skin is coated in green. Season with salt and pepper and roast in a preheated oven 220°C for 15–20 minutes.

When done, take from the oven and add the remaining olive oil to the roasting trays. Rest for 10 minutes so that some pan juices form.

Dress the fennel with these juices and serve it with the guinea fowl along with some crisp parmesan potatoes.

SEARED VEAL CUTLET WITH SAGE

The veal we use at The Restaurant Manfredi is grown specifically for us on a property called Rosemere in western New South Wales. Unlike European white veal, it's redder in colour and more highly flavoured. This is because the calf is not penned but allowed to follow its mother around as she eats grass. Choose the best veal possible for this dish.

Ingredients

extra virgin olive oil
salt and pepper
one veal cutlet per person, trimmed of all fat
plenty of fresh sage leaves
fresh tomato and basil sauce (page 27)

Method

In a heavy skillet pan heat the oil until it is very hot. Season the cutlets on each side then place them in the pan. Place the sage leaves in the pan as well and fry till they are a deep olive green. This should take only about 20 seconds. Be careful not to burn them. Keep them aside.

Turn the cutlets over and sear the other side, then turn the heat down and finish cooking slowly. Throw the oil out of the pan and add some tomato and basil sauce.

Rest in a warm place for about 10 minutes, then serve with the fried sage leaves on top.

LASAGNA OF PRAWNS, MUSSELS, LEEK AND EGGPLANT

SERVES 6 AS FIRST COURSE

Ingredients

2 eggplant, sliced thinly and salted

extra virgin olive oil

12 large king prawns, cooked, peeled, tails left on

1.5 kg mussels, steamed and taken out of their shells

2 cups fresh tomato sauce (page 26)

12 lasagne sheets each 4 cm x 6 cm, rolled thin (see pasta method, page 30)

2 large leeks, thoroughly washed and outer leaves discarded

Method

Spread the slices of eggplant in a baking tray and sprinkle with olive oil. Bake in a moderate oven until they are soft. Slice the leeks thinly and cook until soft in a little olive oil.

Simmer the prawns and mussels in the tomato sauce until they are hot. Don't overcook them.

Meanwhile, cook the pasta sheets in plenty of salted boiling water until *al dente*. Place one sheet in the centre of each plate, then on top, some slices of eggplant, then two prawns, then leek and mussels. Finally, use the other lasagne sheet to cover the lot.

FRITTATA WITH LEEKS AND BASIL

This is a traditional frittata, cooked at high heat and not finished in the oven. It should be creamy and sweet in the centre, and slightly charred on the top and bottom.

SERVES 4 AS A SNACK

Ingredients

7 eggs
a handful of grated parmesan
a few fresh basil leaves
olive oil
1 leek, chopped into rounds
salt and pepper

Method

Crack eggs into a bowl. Beat lightly then add parmesan and basil. Heat oil and add the leeks, cooking until soft. Turn up heat, then add egg mixture and cook, lifting the edges as they cook with a spatula. Turn the frittata and cook the other side.

BEANS, ASPARAGUS AND FRIED PROSCIUTTO SALAD

SERVES 6 FOR A FIRST COURSE

Ingredients

200 g green beans, stems removed
500 g asparagus
extra virgin olive oil
1 clove garlic, minced
handful parsley, chopped
6 slices prosciutto

Method

Cook beans and asparagus in plenty of salted boiling water until *al dente*. Drain and dress immediately with the olive oil, garlic and chopped parsley.

Fry the prosciutto in a small amount of olive oil until it is crisp. When it has cooled enough, crumble it over the beans and asparagus as a final dressing, then serve.

PASTA STRACCI WITH BROOK TROUT AND SICILIAN CAPER SALSA

Brook trout is a big (up to 2 kg) full-flavoured freshwater fish, originally from Canada. Bred in the Lachlan River near Orange, it has an earthy, grainy flavour and texture, and a bright orange flesh. Substitute any of the trout, or even salmon.

SERVES 6 AS A FIRST COURSE

For the caper salsa

MAKES ABOUT 2 CUPS

Ingredients

1 celery heart, cut into small dice
1 roast red capsicum, skinned and diced
1 roast yellow capsicum, skinned and diced
flesh of 1 tomato, seeded and diced
1/2 medium red onion, diced
2 tablespoons Aeolian capers
4 tablespoons extra virgin olive oil
salt and pepper to taste

Method

Mix the diced ingredients together in a bowl with the capers and olive oil. Season and allow to marinate for about $1/2$ hour.

For the brook trout

1 brook trout weighing 500–600 g

Method
After filleting the trout and removing the little bones from the centre with tweezers, slice the flesh very thinly and lay the pieces on a large plate, ready for use. (The trout will be served raw.)

To make the pasta
Make a well with about 500 g plain flour. Add enough whole eggs so that, when they are worked into the flour, the dough is not sticky and not dry. Compensate by adding more flour if too sticky, or more egg if not dry.

Cut the pasta dough into smaller workable pieces so that it can easily be passed through your pasta machine. Roll it till you have sheets that are quite thin. Cut the rolled sheets into random shapes to resemble small pieces of rag or *stracci*. Lay them on a well-floured board until needed.

To assemble the dish
To a large pot about three-quarters full of water, add a large pinch of salt and bring to the boil. Add the *pasta stracci* and cook until *al dente*. Drain and put the pasta in a large bowl with some of the caper salsa and the raw brook trout. Toss well and serve immediately.

SEARED DUCK LIVERS WITH FRIED PROSCIUTTO AND PARMESAN POTATOES

You can use fried prosciutto in a number of ways — fried and left whole, as in this dish, or crumbled and sprinkled over a salad as a seasoning.

SERVES 6 AS A MAIN COURSE

Parmesan potatoes

Ingredients

3 Desiree potatoes, peeled and sliced into thin rounds
olive oil
3/4 cup grated parmesan

Method

Preheat the oven at 220°C.

Brush the surface of a heavy baking tray with olive oil. Place the potato slices on the tray and brush them with olive oil as well. Sprinkle each slice with parmesan and cook in the oven for 4 minutes. Turn the slices over and return to oven until they are golden. Watch them carefully as they cook quickly.

The livers

Ingredients

allow 4–5 duck livers per person
12 large slices prosciutto
300 g green beans, topped, tailed and blanched until *al dente*
olive oil
6 tablespoons veal stock
balsamic vinegar
salt and pepper to taste

Method

Heat some olive oil in a frypan and fry the prosciutto until crisp. Drain on absorbent paper. Heat more olive oil in another frypan and sauté the livers gently until pink. Deglaze the pan with the veal stock and the balsamic vinegar. Season to taste. Place the prosciutto on top of the livers and serve with the beans and parmesan potatoes.

MEDITERRANEAN TUNA

Here we find all the flavours associated with the Mediterranean on one plate. Even though some of the best tuna in the world comes from Sicily, Australian tuna is equally good — and probably cleaner.

SERVES 6 AS A LARGE COURSE

Ingredients

1 medium eggplant, cut into thin slices
olive oil
1 cup tomato and olive oil sauce (page 27)
2 red capsicum, roasted, peeled and cut into 1-cm-wide strips
6 tablespoons anchovy and roast garlic paste (page 72)
6 tablespoons pesto (see page 28)
6 tuna steaks, cut about 1 cm thick
salt and pepper to taste
6 teaspoons Aeolian capers, salt washed off

Method

Place the eggplant slices on a tea towel and sprinkle salt on both sides. Leave for 10 minutes, then pat dry. In a pan, heat some olive oil and fry the eggplant until they are golden brown. Set aside until they are needed.

Spoon tomato sauce onto serving plates, add 4–5 eggplant slices and 4–5 slices of roast capsicum. Spoon on the roast garlic in little piles and scatter the pesto as well.

In a frypan heat some olive oil and sear each of the tuna steaks on both sides until they are pink in the middle. Season and put one on each of the prepared plates. Sprinkle on the capers and serve immediately.

STINGRAY BRAISED IN TOMATO AND FENNEL

Stingray, known as skate here, is one of the most underrated fish in Australia. Its highly gelatinous flesh lends itself very well to braising or poaching.

SERVES 6–8 AS A FIRST COURSE

Ingredients
1.5 kg skate, cut into 6 or 8 pieces
1 fennel bulb, trimmed and cut into thin slices
1 onion, sliced thin
2 garlic cloves, minced
6–8 ripe tomatoes, chopped
4 tablespoons olive oil
salt and pepper to taste

Method
In a wide pan heat the olive oil on a moderate flame and add the onions, garlic and fennel. Fry gently for about 5 minutes, keeping them stirred, until the vegetables soften. Add the tomatoes and simmer for another 5 minutes. Now distribute the skate evenly through the pan, put the lid on, and turn the heat down to a low simmer for about 10–15 minutes.

You can tell if the skate is cooked by pulling some of the flesh aside with a knife and fork to reveal the middle. Season with salt and pepper and serve hot or cold with lots of salad and crusty bread.

Option
Add some black olives for extra flavour.

ROAST BEEF WITH ASPARAGUS AND PARMESAN

SERVES 4 AS A MAIN COURSE

Ingredients

1-kg piece of beef sirloin, rump or butt fillet, trimmed of all fat
500 g fresh asparagus, with the tough ends removed
4 tablespoons extra virgin olive oil
100 g parmesan cheese, cut into large, thin shavings
freshly ground pepper

Method

Preheat the oven to 240°C. Rub the beef with a little olive oil and sprinkle freshly ground pepper over it. Place the beef in a roasting pan and roast in the oven for 15 minutes. Take the meat out and let it 'rest' in its tray.

Meanwhile, bring some water to the boil in a saucepan large enough to hold the asparagus (they can be cut in half if they are too long). Throw the asparagus into the boiling water for 1 minute only. They should be cooked but still be slightly crunchy.

Slice the beef into thin pieces and put them onto plates. Collect the juices that have come from the meat and mix them with the olive oil. Place the asparagus on top of the slices of beef, dress this with the olive oil mixture and then sprinkle the parmesan on top.

SPRING VEGETABLE MINESTRONE

The classic Italian soup, usually done in winter as a rich heavy dish, is included here to take advantage of the fresh spring vegetables in a much lighter and cleaner form.

SERVES 12 AT LEAST AS A FIRST COURSE

Ingredients

1 veal shank (optional), trimmed of all fat
1/4 cabbage, sliced in strips about 1 cm thick
2 potatoes, peeled and cut into chunks
1 carrot, peeled and cut into 1-cm-thick rounds
2 sticks celery, cut into rounds
3 ripe tomatoes, roughly chopped
8 cloves garlic, peeled and left whole
1 handful each parsley and basil leaves
1 cup shelled peas
1/2 cup broad beans, shelled and peeled
salt and pepepr to taste

Method

In a pot large enough to hold everything and two-thirds filled with cold water, place the shank, cabbage, potatoes, carrot, celery, tomatoes, garlic, parsley and basil. Place the pot on the heat, bring to the boil then turn down to a simmer for 30 minutes. Add the peas and beans, simmer for a further 10 minutes then season. Serve with grated cheese and crusty bread.

WARM TRIPE SALAD WITH ROAST ESCHALLOTS

This dish was suggested to me by my friend, Michael Langley, himself a gifted cook. He told me he loved tripe, loved the way we do it in The Restaurant Manfredi, but asked was it possible to do something more modern with it. How about a tripe salad, he suggested. The more I thought about it, the more sense it made. The texture of tripe is perfect with crunchy salad vegetables. Here is that dish. He was the first to try it, loved it, and it's been in our repertoire ever since.

SERVES 8 AS A MAIN COURSE

Ingredients

2 pieces cooked honeycomb tripe

500 g eschallots

2 heads radicchio, washed and dried

2 bulbs fennel, cut into thin wedges

some rucola, washed and dried

1 head witlof, separated into its leaves

extra virgin olive oil

red wine vinegar

salt and pepper

Method

Place the tripe in a pot, cover with cold water, bring to the boil and simmer for about 20 minutes. Drain, allow to cool then slice into bite-sized strips.

Place the eschallots on a roasting tray, sprinkle with olive oil and salt and roast in a preheated oven at 180°C for 15–20 minutes until soft. Peel away the skin and reserve.

Heat a little olive oil in a pan and fry the pieces of tripe until they become crispy. Season and reserve.

Put all the salad leaves, fennel and eschallots in a bowl and dress with olive oil and vinegar. Season and serve with the crisp tripe.

MULBERRY AND ALMOND PIE

MAKES 16 INDIVIDUAL TARTS

For the pastry

Ingredients

175 g plain flour

1/4 teaspoon baking powder

pinch salt

65 g caster sugar

125 g chilled butter

1 egg yolk

Method

Mix together the flour, baking powder, salt and sugar. Work in the butter and the egg quickly. Rest in refrigerator for at least 1 hour. Line tart shells with the pastry and blind bake at 180°C for 10–15 minutes. They should be slightly undercooked.

For the filling

Ingredients

4 eggs
240 g caster sugar
1/2 teaspoon vanilla extract
1/2 teaspoon almond extract
zest of 1 lemon
300 g almond meal
allow 10–15 mulberries per tart

Method

Mix all the ingredients, except for the almond meal and the mulberries, together in a bowl using a wooden spoon. It is important to use a mixing action and not a folding action. Now incorporate the almond meal into the mixture.

Scatter the mulberries on the bottom of the prepared tart cases and pour the mixture over them. Cook in a moderate oven 180°C–200°C till the tarts are golden brown. This should take 12–15 minutes. Serve with vanilla gelato or fresh cream.

PEACH AND PLUM TORTA

SERVES 10

The sponge

Ingredients

8 eggs
160 g icing sugar
160 g plain flour, sieved
60 g melted butter

Method

Beat the eggs and sugar together over a low flame until they are just warm. Take away from the heat and beat until they triple in volume. Fold in the flour and butter.

Pour into two 18 cm x 25 cm sponge tins and bake for 18 minutes at 180°C.

Assembly

Ingredients

1 cup hazelnut liqueur (Frangelico)
1/3 cup sugar syrup (mix with the liqueur)
300 g mascarpone
2 peaches, sliced
3–4 plums, sliced

Method

Cut the sponge into 3 pieces to fit into a rectangular bread mould. Place the first piece of sponge on the bottom of the mould and liberally brush on the liqueur. Cover with a layer of mascarpone, then place the peach slices in neat rows to cover the mascarpone. Repeat for the next layer using the second piece of sponge and the plums, then cover with the final piece of sponge, brushing this one as well with the liqueur.

Place something flat and heavy over the top and leave to set a couple of hours in the refrigerator. Slice and serve.

ROAST SUCKLING LEG OF LAMB WITH ROSEMARY AND ROAST POTATOES

The suckling lamb we use at The Restaurant Manfredi, Illabo lamb, comes from Tony Lehmann's property near Junee in western New South Wales. One of the problems we used to have in The Restaurant Manfredi was inconsistency in the quality of meat supplied — in Europe you would deal with a single producer rather than a wholesaler. So a group of us approached Tony and, over the years, working together, we have developed this product, which is now of consistently excellent quality. We buy anything from six to eight lambs a week, and butcher them in our kitchen. If suckling lamb is not available, first ask your butcher why not and, second, choose the smallest spring lamb legs.

SERVES 6 AS A MAIN COURSE

Ingredients
2 suckling lamb legs, trimmed of any excess flap
1/4 cup olive oil
1 bunch rosemary
2 kg potatoes, peeled and cut into bite-sized pieces
salt and pepper

Method
Rub the lamb legs with some of the olive oil and season well with salt and pepper. Place in a baking dish on sprigs of rosemary and roast in a preheated oven at 220°C for 20–25 minutes. Remove the lamb from the oven and place in a warm place to rest for about 20 minutes.

For the potatoes, place them in a baking tray and sprinkle generously with olive oil. Add a couple of sprigs of rosemary. Season well with salt and pepper and toss them so they are completely covered with oil. Roast in the oven at the same temperature as the lamb leg. The potatoes should also take about 20–25 minutes. Pinkeye potatoes take a little longer to cook than other potatoes.

Slice the lamb legs and serve with the roast potatoes and some of the juices released by the meat.

RHUBARB PUDDING

MAKES 10 INDIVIDUAL PUDDINGS

The brioche

Ingredients

400 ml milk
60 g fresh yeast
12 egg yolks
1 kg flour
300 g unsalted butter

Method

Heat the milk to blood temperature and dissolve the yeast in it. Add the yolks. Place the flour in a mixer and add the liquid while beating slowly. Now add the butter in 50-g pieces. Transfer to a large bowl and place somewhere warm until it rises to double its original size. Knead well and then place in loaf tins. Bake at 180°C for 20–25 minutes.

The rhubarb

Ingredients

4 bunches rhubarb, cleaned and cut into pieces
600 g raspberries
200 g sugar
juice 1 lemon
500 g strawberries, chopped into small dice

Method

Simmer all the ingredients until the rhubarb breaks down, mixing occasionally so it does not burn.

To assemble

Cut the brioche into pieces that fit the inside of the moulds you are using. Spoon some of the mixture in then put another piece of brioche in. Repeat procedure until the mould is full. Finish with a piece of brioche then spoon some rhubarb on. Allow to set in the refrigerator with a weight on them. This way they will soak up more of the rhubarb.

VENISON CUTLET WITH FRESH TOMATO AND BASIL SAUCE

The sauce

Ingredients

1.5 kg ripe tomatoes, peeled and seeded
1 cup fresh basil leaves, torn into small pieces
3 garlic cloves, peeled and minced
6 tablespoons good olive oil
freshly ground pepper
salt

Method

To peel the tomatoes, place them in a pot of boiling water for 30 seconds then transfer them to a bowl of cold water. The skin should peel away quite easily using small knife. Cut the peeled tomatoes in half and squeeze out the seeds from the centre. Now chop them into small pieces and, making sure you collect the juice, place them in a bowl. Add the basil, garlic and oil. Season with the salt and pepper and mix thoroughly. Let it rest for at least $\frac{1}{2}$ hour.

The venison

Ingredients

allow one venison cutlet per person, trimmed
breadcrumbs
handful grated parmesan
1 egg, beaten
plain flour
olive oil
salt and pepper

Method

Mix the breadcrumbs with the parmesan and season with salt and pepper. Dust each cutlet with flour, dip in the egg and then coat with the breadcrumb mixture. In a skillet, heat some oil then lightly brown the cutlets. Place in a baking tray and place in a hot 250°C preheated oven for 10–12 minutes. Take them out, rest for 10 more minutes then serve with boiled, sliced potatoes and the sauce.

STRAWBERRY AND MASCARPONE SOFFIATI

SERVES 6

The soffiati

Ingredients

250 ml water
60 g butter
250 g flour
4 eggs
pinch salt

Method

Bring the water, butter and salt slowly to the boil. Remove from the heat, sift in the flour and work mixture over moderate heat until a thin crust forms on the bottom of the saucepan. Transfer mixture to a clean saucepan and rest for two minutes.

Add eggs one at a time, beating each in thoroughly with a wooden spoon before adding the next. Pipe the mixture into 12 small mounds on a baking tray and sprinkle lightly with water before baking in a preheated oven at 220°C for 20 minutes. Cook on a cake rack.

The sauce

Ingredients

100 g sugar
100 ml water
250 g strawberries

Method

Heat the sugar and water together, stirring until the sugar has totally dissolved. Cool. Puree the berries in a food processor, then sieve. Add the sugar syrup to taste.

Assembly

250 g mascarpone
500 g strawberries, topped and halved
icing sugar

Cut the pastries in half, spread a layer of mascarpone on the bottom halves and fill with strawberries. Dust the tops with icing sugar and set in place. Arrange on plates with the sauce and the remaining berries and serve.

December to February

Vegetables

lettuce (Cos, iceberg, mignonette)	Cucumber
Sweet corn	Capsicum
Tomatoes	String beans (all beans are abundant now)
Zucchini	Chillis

Fruit

Melons	Nectarines
Persimmon (available late summer)	Apricots
Figs	Peaches
Berries start now	Passionfruit
Lychees	Plums
Mangoes	Melons (rockmelons, watermelons)
Cherries	Pineapples

THE BOLD AND GUTSY TASTE OF summer is at its best in the tomato — ripe from the hot sun, bursting with juice and flavour. Peel them, puree them, push the pulp through a sieve, mix it with olive oil, dribble pesto all over it and chill it: summer in a bowl.

Walk into a fruit shop and you're overwhelmed by the fragrance of the stone fruit: peaches, nectarines and, every three or four years, apricots worth eating. And melons and cherries — and in late January we get figs from Tenterfield, black ones, rich and oozing with soaked-up sunshine. Serve them crunchy: dip them whole in caramelised sugar and let them dry. And, of course, mango, a taste that can't be improved on. Best leave them alone — just peel and eat.

Summer is a time for quick cooking techniques; nobody wants to be cooped up in a hot kitchen. Summer is lots of leaves and lots of fresh food — if you are going to roast capsicum, roast them by the dozen and store them cold.

In Sydney we have the sweet little harbour prawns, another summer taste. We do them in a frittata with basil. In a good season, the yabbies arrive. Throw them into vigorously boiling water; when the water reaches boiling again take them out, plunge them into cold water, pull their heads off, peel the tail and discard the waste. You're left with the tail meat and the sweet meat in the nippers. Use them in a salad, with good oil and capers.

Capers! The best are preserved in salt from the Aeolian Islands. Use them in salads, or to dress a carpaccio. Another summer speciality: roast golf ball chillies slowly, then fill them with anchovies, roast garlic and capers. Do a lot and store them in olive oil. I have a friend who eats capers as a snack while watching the cricket. Another of the tastes of summer.

And here, it's truffle time, imported fresh from a French or Italian winter. The white ones first, air-freighted, wrapped in calico, around $3000 a kilo. This is a problem — a truffle the width of a 50 cent coin will cost a hundred dollars. When we put *spaghetti a la chitarra* on the menu at $30 a bowl, we really only cover costs. We store these precious fungi in arborio rice, then use the rice for truffle risotto, and do the same with eggs — the rice and the eggs absorb the powerful odour. There's nothing to compare with scrambled truffled eggs.

And naturally there is ice-cream. *Gelati, sorbetti, tartufi, cassate. Cassata* means case or drawer, and is a moulded desert; *tartufo* is truffle, here meaning chocolate; *sorbetto* is a water-based ice confection, from the Arabic *sharba* meaning a drink; and *gelato* simply means frozen. All of them mean summer.

We make a *tartufo* with vanilla ice-cream filled with chunks of Italian nougat, set in small, rounded individual servings with chocolate on the edge and sprinkled with roasted coconut threads. I love ice-cream. Once, we served individual *gelati* at a wedding, in tiny cones.

Late summer, the best of the blood plums arrive. We roll them in a sponge with rich vanilla custard speckled with vanilla beans and set the lot in a terrine mould, ready to be sliced.

SUMMER RECIPES

Spicy Tasmanian vongole and mussel soup
Roast eggplant, peperonata and bocconcini
Yabbie and king prawn cannelloni
Tasmanian smoked salmon lasagne
Taglierini with spanner crab, tomato and chilli sauce
Pan fried Sydney rock oysters with a rucola and dried tomato salad
Seared veal steak with capsicum and eggplant sformato
Roast garfish fillets with roast garlic and caper dressing
Summer berry tiers
Blood plum sponge with roast almond gelato
Cherry millefoglie
Artichoke hearts pan fried with parmesan
Barbecued suckling lamb cutlets with a fresh tomato and basil sauce
Roast leeks with mozzarella and parmesan
Fried corzetti with avocado and sorrel
Mussels with a parsley and garlic salsa
Ocean trout and tuna carpaccio rolls
Prawn broth with cuttlefish and black taglierini
Prawn broth with prawn and leek squares
Roast lamb loin salad with leeks
Harbour prawns and basil frittata
Deep fried zucchini flowers and Tasmanian gruyere
Seared cuttlefish with sweet onions and rucola
Tagliatelle with harbour prawns and leeks
Peach and ginger dome
Peach and raspberry sponge

SUMMER — DECEMBER TO FEBRUARY

SUMMER MENU

Spicy Tasmanian vongole and mussel soup
Roast eggplant, peperonata and bocconcini
Seared veal steak with capsicum and eggplant sformato
Blood plum sponge with roast almond gelato

Pan fried Sydney rock oysters with a rucola
and dried tomato salad
Tasmanian smoked salmon lasagne
Roast lamb loin salad with leeks
Summer berry tiers

Prawn broth with cuttlefish and black taglierini
Ocean trout and tuna carpaccio rolls
Yabbie and king prawn cannelloni
Barbecued suckling lamb cutlets with a fresh tomato
and basil sauce
Peach and raspberry sponge

Mussels with a parsley and garlic salsa
Taglierini with spanner crab, tomato and chilli sauce
Roast garfish fillets with roast garlic and caper dressing
Cherry millefoglia

Deep fried zucchini flowers with Tasmanian gruyere
Seared cuttlefish with sweet onions and rucola
Tagliatelle with harbour prawns and leeks
Peach and ginger dome

SPICY TASMANIAN VONGOLE AND MUSSEL SOUP

With this dish, I wanted to get as close as possible to a Thai-style soup, without using Asian ingredients. There is nothing in this recipe you couldn't find in an Italian market. Australian cooks are influenced by Asian food — this is my way of being influenced. Vongole are baby clams.

MAKES ENOUGH BROTH FOR 12–15 PEOPLE

Ingredients

prawn shells from 3 kg cooked prawns
2 celery sticks, cut into chunks
1 carrot, cut into rounds
2 leeks, chopped
6–8 ripe tomatoes, peeled and chopped
1/2 cup parsley, roughly chopped
1 leek, cut into fine julienne strips
handful basil leaves
6 red long chillies, chopped
6 mussels per portion, cleaned and beard removed
10 vongole per portion

Method

Place the prawn shells, celery, carrot, chopped leeks and tomatoes in a pot. Cover with plenty of cold fresh water and bring to a simmer. Keep simmering for 1–1$^{1}/_{2}$ hours then strain. Reduce it by half, then season to taste.

To finish the soup, add the leek strips, basil, chillies, mussels and vongole to the broth and simmer until the mussels and vongole have opened. Take the meat out of their shells, distribute among the serving plates, season the soup and serve.

ROAST EGGPLANT, PEPERONATA AND BOCCONCINI

I was on holiday in Bali, and had been two weeks without cooking. The cook at our resort had invited some friends from another resort for lunch, and jokingly asked if I'd like to help. I jumped at the chance. This is one of the dishes I made up from available ingredients.

SERVES 4 AS A FIRST COURSE

The eggplant

Ingredients

1–2 medium eggplants, cut into 1-cm-thick slices
olive oil
salt

Method

Sprinkle a little salt on both sides of each slice of eggplant. Wait 10 minutes then pat each slice dry with a towel. Brush each slice with the olive oil, place on a baking tray and roast in the oven at 220°C until the eggplant is golden brown. Allow to cool.

The peperonata

Ingredients

2 large red capsicum, cut into large pieces
2 medium onions, cut into chunks
4 egg tomatoes, roughly chopped
handful of basil
2 cloves garlic, minced
6 tablespoons extra virgin olive oil
salt and pepper to taste

Method

In a large saucepan heat the olive oil. Add the capsicum, onion and garlic. Turn up the heat, fry and keep stirring with a wooden spoon for a couple of minutes until the contents wilt a little. Add the tomatoes and simmer for 20 minutes, stirring occasionally. Add the basil, season and allow to cool.

To assemble the sandwich
4 bocconcini (fresh mozzarella balls), sliced thinly

On each plate place an eggplant slice, spoon some of the peperonata on, then add some slices of mozzarella. Now another eggplant slice, some more peperonata, mozzarella and finally a slice of eggplant. You should have a stack like a double decker sandwich. *Buon appetito*.

YABBIE AND KING PRAWN CANNELLONI

SERVES 6 AS A FIRST COURSE

Pasta
Make the cannelloni by following the basic pasta recipe on page 29.

Ingredients
3 leeks, cleaned, washed and cut into thin rounds
pasta, rolled out into thin sheets
750 g green king prawns, peeled, deveined
500 g yabbies, cooked and peeled
2 cups fresh tomato and basil sauce (page 27)
1 cup grated mozzarella cheese
1/3 cup grated parmesan cheese
olive oil
salt and pepper to taste

Method
Heat some olive oil in a pan and gently fry the leeks until they are soft.

Cut the sheets of pasta into 12 rectangles 6 cm by 10 cm. Cook immediately in plenty of fast boiling, salted water. Place the cooked sheets onto wet tea towels.

Lightly fry the prawns in a little olive oil in a frypan.

Spoon some of the leeks onto each sheet of pasta, then 1–1½ prawns. Now roll the cannelloni like a cigarette.

Spoon some of the tomato sauce onto the bottom of a baking dish. Arrange the cannelloni in the dish, distribute the tomato sauce on top, then the mozzarella and parmesan. Season and place in a preheated oven at 170°C for 15 minutes. Serve hot with a yabbie tail on top.

TASMANIAN SMOKED SALMON LASAGNA

This dish represents a turning point in my development as a cook. It showed me I could break out of my cultural restraints (Cold lasagna! Unheard of, say Italian patrons before they try it) and allow other influences to wash over me. On the other hand, my wife Julie reckons she said it was time I did something different — and this dish was the result.

SERVES 10 AS A FIRST COURSE

Parsley and garlic salsa

Ingredients

large bunch of Italian or flat leaf parsley
2–3 cloves garlic, peeled
extra virgin olive oil
sea salt
freshly ground pepper

Method

Place the parsley and garlic in a food processor. Turn it on, dribbling the olive oil in a little at a time until you have a textured but still runny salsa. Season.

Assembly

Ingredients

500 g sliced, smoked Tasmanian salmon
various tender young garden greens (rucola, sorrel, lamb's tongue)
fresh tomato and olive oil sauce (page 27)
parsley and garlic salsa (above)
3 sheets each white and black pasta (page 29), cut exactly
   to the size of the terrine mould
extra virgin olive oil

Method

Brush some olive oil on the inside of a flat-sided terrine mould. Lay a sheet of black pasta on the bottom. Spoon some parsley salsa on top and spread it out thinly with the back of a spoon. Lay slices of smoked salmon over so that they cover the pasta completely. Now lay a sheet of the white pasta on top and spoon some tomato sauce over. Spread it evenly then lay on some of the garden leaves. You can be fairly generous with these because their fresh flavour and texture will provide contrast to the other rich ingredients in the lasagna.

Repeat the sequence of layers until you have used up all the pasta sheets. There should be two layers of greens and three layers of smoked salmon. Oil the top sheet then cover and refrigerate.

To serve, turn it out onto a flat tray and slice into appropriate pieces.

TAGLIERINI WITH SPANNER CRAB, TOMATO AND CHILLI SAUCE

SERVES 6 AS A FIRST COURSE

Tomato and chilli sauce

Ingredients

2 leeks, cleaned and cut into rounds
2 chillies, seeded and chopped
2 cloves garlic, minced
extra virgin olive oil
2 kg ripe tomatoes, peeled and chopped
basil leaves
salt and pepper

Method

Fry the leeks, chillies and garlic in the olive oil until they have softened. Add the tomatoes and simmer for 10–15 minutes. Add the basil and season. The sauce is now ready to use.

Taglierini

Ingredients

360 g cooked spanner crab meat
pasta cut to taglierini size (page 30)
tomato and chilli sauce (above)
handful freshly grated parmesan cheese

Method

Cook the taglierini in plenty of rapidly boiling water. Drain well, distribute evenly among the serving bowls, add the spanner crab and tomato and chilli sauce and toss. It should be served immediately with freshly grated parmesan.

PAN FRIED SYDNEY ROCK OYSTERS WITH A RUCOLA AND DRIED TOMATO SALAD

Chopped dried tomatoes are wonderful as a seasoning over salad, fish, even meats and vegetables.

SERVES 6 AS A FIRST COURSE

Ingredients

1 medium eggplant, cut into 1 cm x 3 cm pieces
extra virgin olive oil
2 red capsicum, roasted, peeled and sliced into strips
6 handfuls young rucola leaves, washed and dried
12 dried tomatoes, chopped into small dice
36 Sydney rock oysters, taken out of their shells
1/2 cup grated parmesan
salt and pepper to taste

Method

Pan fry the eggplant pieces in olive oil until they have softened. Put them in a large bowl with the capsicum, *rucola* and dried tomatoes. Dress with a little olive oil, season and arrange on the serving plates.

Toss the oysters in the grated parmesan, heat some olive oil in a frypan and fry oysters quickly at high heat on both sides. Place the oysters on top of the salad and serve.

SEARED VEAL STEAK WITH CAPSICUM AND EGGPLANT SFORMATO

A *sformato* is the Italian equivalent of a *timbale* — anything that is moulded and turned out of a mould.

SERVES 6 AS A MAIN COURSE

Ingredients

24 slices veal from the loin about 1/2 cm thick
2 large red capsicum, roasted, peeled and cut in 6 pieces, lengthways
1 medium eggplant, sliced into thin rounds
6 bocconcini, cut into small dice
4–5 leeks, cleaned and cut into 1/2-cm rounds
1/4 cup veal stock
olive oil
salt and pepper to taste

Method

To make the *sformati* we need 6 small souffle moulds about 9 cm in diameter and 4 cm deep.

Fry the eggplant slices in olive oil until they brown lightly, then drain them on absorbent paper. Also fry the leeks in olive oil until they soften. Line the base and sides of the moulds alternately with eggplant and red capsicum. Mix the leeks and bocconcini together and season. Fill the moulds with this mixture, then place a slice of eggplant on top to close the *sformato*, tucking in any capsicum or eggplant hanging over.

To reheat when needed, place mould in a water bath in a preheated 120°C oven for 10 minutes. The contents will drop out of the mould and onto the serving plate very easily.

To cook the veal, heat some olive oil in a frypan until it is just smoking. Fry the veal pieces quickly on both sides, then immediately season and place on the serving plates with the *sformato*.

Deglaze the pan with the veal stock and reduce to the desired thickness. Turn off the heat and add a few drops of extra virgin olive oil. Add sauce evenly to the dishes and serve.

ROAST GARFISH FILLETS WITH ROAST GARLIC AND CAPER DRESSING

SERVES 6 AS MAIN COURSE

Roast garlic paste

Ingredients

4 garlic bulbs left whole, unpeeled
6 tablespoons extra virgin olive oil
salt and pepper to taste

Method

Roast the whole garlic bulbs, on a tray, in a preheated oven at 100°C for 30–45 minutes until they are soft. Cut the bulbs in half and squeeze the garlic out like toothpaste into a bowl. Mash with a fork, add the olive oil, season and mix thoroughly. The paste is now ready to use.

To finish

Ingredients

12 garfish fillets
6 tablespoons dried tomatoes, chopped into small dice
3 bunches asparagus, trimmed and cooked *al dente*
12 tablespoons garlic paste (above)
1 cup caper salsa (page 108)
6 small Desiree potatoes, boiled *al dente* and sliced into ½-cm rounds
olive oil
salt and pepper to taste

Method

Lay the garfish fillets flat and place 1 tablespoon of garlic paste on each. Roll the fillets up and secure the end with a toothpick.

Place 12 potato slices on a baking dish and place the garfish fillets on the potato slices. Cover the top of each fillet with ½ tablespoon of the chopped dried tomatoes.

Sprinkle with olive oil, season and roast in a 220°C preheated oven for 15 minutes. Arrange on the plate with the asparagus and add the caper dressing. Serve immediately.

SUMMER BERRY TIERS

SERVES 8–10

The tiers biscuits

Ingredients

240 g egg whites (egg whites from seven 61 g eggs)
400 g caster sugar
200 g butter, melted at room temperature
1/2 teaspoon pure vanilla essence
240 g plain flour
60 g cocoa

Method

Whisk egg whites and sugar together to soft peak stage. Fold in the vanilla and melted butter. Sift the flour and cocoa together then mix these in as well.

Spoon onto buttered baking tray (spread in a thin circle) and bake in a preheated 160°C oven until they have darkened slightly. Take them off the tray immediately and allow to cool completely. Can be stored in an airtight container.

The custard cream

Ingredients

2 vanilla beans, slit and scraped
1200 ml single cream
300 g caster sugar
20 egg yolks

Method

Place the vanilla beans and cream in a saucepan and bring to the boil. Cream the sugar and egg yolks together until they form a ribbon.* Whisk this into the hot cream. Cook in a bain marie or on a low heat (80°C) until the custard thickens.

Assembly

Have as many different berries as possible on hand. On each plate place a tier biscuit then spread on some of the custard cream and scatter the different berries on in one layer. The strawberries may have to be cut in half. Repeat this, building up the tier, finishing off with a biscuit dusted with icing sugar on top.

BLOOD PLUM SPONGE WITH ROAST ALMOND GELATO

MAKES 1 TERRINE SERVING 8–10

For the sponge

Ingredients

6 egg yolks
75 g caster sugar
6 egg whites
150 g caster sugar
80 g plain flour, sifted

Method

Cream the yolks and first amount of caster sugar until they are thick and fluffy. Whip the egg whites and second amount of sugar together until they form soft peaks. Now fold the two mixtures and the flour together. Spread onto two rectangular baking sheets and bake in a preheated oven at 180°C till just *under-cooked*.

---

* For explanation, see page 38

Soaking syrup

Ingredients

1/2 cup sugar syrup
1/2 cup grappa

Method

Combine these and mix well.

Serving syrup

Ingredients

750 ml dessert wine — botrytis riesling or semillon
250 g caster sugar
1 vanilla pod, slit in half lengthways

Method

Place all ingredients in a saucepan and reduce by about half. Allow to cool.

Roast almond gelato

Ingredients

400 g whole raw almonds, skin on
1 litre single cream
200 g sugar
8 egg yolks

Method

Roast the almonds in a 150°–170°C oven until slightly coloured (about 6–8 minutes). Cool, then pound in a bag or cloth until they are broken into small pieces. Make a *crema inglese* with the rest of the ingredients, cool and churn. Add the roasted almond pieces and mix into the gelato. Freeze.

Assembly

Ingredients

12 sweet, ripe but firm blood plums, cut in half, stone removed
1 litre thick pastry cream (page 140)
sponge, syrups and gelato (see above)

Method

Once the sponges are made, turn them both out onto separate teatowels. Brush them with the soaking syrup and spread the custard evenly over them. Distribute the blood plums on top of the custard and roll both sponges with the help of the teatowels.

Line a terrine (brioche loaf tin) with plastic wrap and place one of the rolls in. Spread some more custard on and place the other roll on top. Store in the refrigerator. Serve with roast almond gelato and the serving syrup.

CHERRY MILLEFOGLIE

SERVES 6

Pastry cream

Ingredients

80 g cornflour
12 egg yolks
500 ml single cream
500 ml milk
200 g sugar
500 ml whipped cream

Method

Add the cornflour to the egg yolks then proceed as for *crema inglese* (page 38) to make a thick pastry cream. Cool, then fold the pastry cream into whipped cream in equal quantities.

Assembly

Ingredients

2 sheets puff pastry 12 cm x 12 cm, each rolled out fairly thin
750 g cherries, pitted
1/2 cup kirsch, 1/2 cup sugar syrup, mixed together
pastry cream as above
icing sugar

Method

Bake the puff pastry, pricking it occasionally so that it doesn't rise too much. After it is cooked to a golden brown, allow to cool completely, then cut each sheet into nine equal squares.

For the filling, soak the cherries in the sugar and kirsch syrup for at least 1 hour.

To assemble, spread a layer of pastry cream on a square of pastry then spoon on some of the cherries. Repeat for the second layer. Dust the final piece of pastry with icing sugar, place on the very top and serve.

ARTICHOKE HEARTS PAN FRIED WITH PARMESAN

SERVE AS A FIRST COURSE

Ingredients

allow 2 or 4 artichokes per person, according to size
grated parmesan cheese
2 lemons
olive oil

For choosing and cooking the artichokes, see recipe for tagliatelle with artichokes and parmesan (page 101).

Method

Once the artichokes have cooled, trim away any tough leaves and slice each artichoke into quarters from top to bottom. Remove any fibrous 'choke' from the centre then fill the leaf layers with a little parmesan. Heat some olive oil in a skillet and fry the artichokes lightly until they are golden. Serve immediately or allow to cool to room temperature.

BARBECUED SUCKLING LAMB CUTLETS WITH A FRESH TOMATO AND BASIL SAUCE

SERVES 6 AS A MAIN COURSE

Ingredients

allow 6–8 cutlets per person, trimmed of all fat
fresh tomato and basil sauce (page 27)
salt and pepper to season

Method

Season the cutlets with salt and pepper. Make sure the barbecue is quite hot but not flaming. Sear the cutlets on each side briefly, then rest them. By resting them for 10 minutes they will 'set' and remain pink. Pile them up in the centre of a serving plate and spoon the tomato and basil sauce around them. They are now ready to serve.

ROAST LEEKS WITH MOZZARELLA AND PARMESAN

SERVES 6 AS A FIRST COURSE

Ingredients

12 leeks, washed and trimmed
24 thin slices fresh mozzarella (bocconcini)
2 cups grated parmesan cheese
olive oil
freshly ground pepper

Method

Trim and wash the leeks thoroughly. Slice them in half, lengthways, and cut pieces in half if they are too long. Place them in a baking dish with a little olive oil on the bottom. The open (or cut) side of the leek should be facing up. Sprinkle this open side with olive oil, making sure that it penetrates the layers of the leek.

Now put some mozzarella and parmesan on top and bake in a moderate oven at about 190°C (about 6–8 minutes). They are ready when they have softened and the cheese has turned golden. Season with freshly ground pepper and serve.

FRIED CORZETTI WITH AVOCADO AND SORREL

SERVES 6 AS A LIGHT FIRST COURSE
For the corzetti (pasta, see page 30)
Ingredients
basic pasta dough (page 29)
generous handful of grated parmesan cheese
olive oil

Method

Once the dough is made take small pieces the size of a thumbnail off the large lump. Keeping your fingers well floured, press each piece onto the work surface with your thumb so that it is roughly round. Cook the *corzetti* in an abundant amount of rapidly boiling, salted water until they are *al dente*. Drain and dress them with olive oil so that they don't stick to one another. Mix in a generous quantity of grated parmesan cheese. Heat a little olive oil in a pan and toss the *corzetti* till golden.

Assembly

Ingredients

1 medium avocado, mashed with a fork
6–8 dried tomatoes, finely chopped
12 sorrel leaves, sliced into fine strips
salt and pepper to season

Method

Mix together the avocado and dried tomatoes and season with salt and pepper. Spoon a little of this mixture between two of the pasta *corzetti*, then spoon a little more on top and cover with another *corzetti*, so that the result is a two-layered 'sandwich' or tier. Wrap the finely sliced sorrel around the exposed sides of the mixture so that it sticks to the mashed avocado. The filled *corzetti* are now ready to serve.

MUSSELS WITH A PARSLEY AND GARLIC SALSA

SERVES 4 AS A FIRST COURSE

Ingredients

10–12 mussels per person, washed and bearded
1 leek, washed and sliced
1/2 cup dry white wine
bunch of Italian or flat-leaf parsley, washed and de-stalked
2 cloves garlic, minced
extra virgin olive oil
salt and pepper

Method

Place the mussels, wine and leek in a covered pot. Turn the heat up to full and steam the mussels open. This should take about 5 minutes. Give the pot a good shake to help the mussels along. Place them on a tray or tip them into the sink to cool.

Meanwhile, place the parsley leaves and garlic in a food processor and turn it on. Dribble the olive oil in a little at a time until the consistency of a thick dressing is achieved.

To serve the mussels, remove the top half of the shell, place on a serving plate and dress with the *salsa*. Season to taste.

OCEAN TROUT AND TUNA CARPACCIO ROLLS

SERVES 6 AS A MAIN COURSE

Ingredients

one side of ocean trout weighing about 300 g, filleted and boned
one piece of tuna weighing about 250 g, preferably cut from the middle
1 celery heart, cut into small dice
1 roast red capsicum, skinned and diced
1 roast yellow capsicum, skinned and diced
flesh of 1 tomato, seeded and diced
1/2 medium red onion, diced
2 tablespoons Aeolian capers
4 tablespoons extra virgin olive oil
salt and pepper

Method

To help slice the fish very finely, place them in the freezer for about an hour. This will firm the flesh so that slicing is easier. Use a very sharp knife to slice rounds of tuna, laying them flat on a tray or plate in the refrigerator. With the trout fillet, slice the pieces in a parallel fashion to the fillet. Don't be alarmed if there are holes in your slices — you will improve with practice. Lay the trout slices on a tray or plate and refrigerate like the tuna.

Mix the diced vegetables together in a bowl along with the capers and olive oil. Season and allow to marinate for about $\frac{1}{2}$ hour. Then take each slice of tuna and trout and place a little of the mixture in the centre. Roll it neatly so it makes a tight tube. Serve them sitting up with some delicate garden greens such as *rucola* or *mizuna*.

PRAWN BROTH WITH CUTTLEFISH AND BLACK TAGLIERINI

MAKES ENOUGH BROTH FOR 10–15 PEOPLE

Ingredients

1.5 kg inky cuttlefish
lots of prawn shells (precooked)
2 celery sticks, chopped into 2-cm rounds
1 carrot, chopped into 2-cm rounds
2 leeks, chopped into 2-cm rounds
6 ripe tomatoes, peeled and chopped
50 g black taglierini per person
parsley, roughly chopped
extra virgin olive oil
salt and pepper

Method

Place prawns, vegetables and tomatoes in a pot. Cover with plenty of cold fresh water and bring to a simmer. Keep simmering for 1–1½ hours, then strain. Reduce if it is not intense enough, then season to taste.

Clean the cuttlefish. Prepare the black *taglierini* as shown on page 30. Bring the prawn broth to the boil and add the *taglierini* and cuttlefish and cook until the pasta is *al dente*. Finish off with the parsley and a spoonful of olive oil.

SUMMER — DECEMBER TO FEBRUARY

PRAWN BROTH WITH PRAWN AND LEEK SQUARES

MAKES ENOUGH BROTH FOR 10–12 PEOPLE

Ingredients

extra virgin olive oil
1 kg prawns, peeled and deveined
2 leeks, finely sliced
2 cloves garlic, minced
salt and pepper
basic pasta rolled into sheets (page 30)
prawn broth (see previous recipe, page 146)

Method

Put some olive oil in a pan and gently fry the prawns, leeks and garlic. Place the contents of the pan into a food processor and blend. Season and allow to cool.

Meanwhile, roll out the pasta sheets. When cooled, spread the prawn and leek mixture on one sheet and place another sheet on top. Use a rolling pin to even out the mixture. Do this gently so that the pasta does not tear. With a pasta cutter, cut the piece into 1-cm squares.

Bring the broth to the boil then cook the little squares until they are done (about 3–5 minutes). Finish by adding a spoonful of good olive oil before serving.

ROAST LAMB LOIN SALAD WITH LEEKS

SERVES 4 AS A FIRST COURSE

Ingredients

trimmed lamb loin, total weight about 500 g
1/4 cup olive oil
200 g green beans, trimmed and blanched
the very tender part of a leek, thinly sliced
salt and pepper

Method

Slice the lamb loin into manageable lengths. In a skillet heat 2–3 tablespoons of the olive oil and sear the loins on each side for about 15 seconds, just long enough to seal them.

Place them immediately in a baking dish, cover lightly with some olive oil and roast in a preheated oven at 200°C for 7–10 minutes. Remove the loins from the baking dish and rest them in a warm place for 10 minutes.

Season and toss the beans together with the sliced leek and the lamb and the remaining olive oil and arrange this salad on a plate. Season and dress with any roasting juices that have been given off, then serve.

HARBOUR PRAWN AND BASIL FRITTATA

MAKES 1 SINGLE SERVE AS A FIRST COURSE

Ingredients

2 eggs
1 tablespoon grated parmesan
10–12 harbour prawns, cooked and peeled
1 handful rucola leaves, thinly sliced
1 tablespoon pesto
olive oil
salt and pepper

Method

Heat a little olive oil in a skillet until it is just smoking. Beat the eggs lightly with the parmesan, season and pour into the hot pan. The *frittata* should be quite wide and spread over the pan quite thinly. It should take only a couple of minutes to cook.

Now distribute the prawns so that they heat on the *frittata*. Transfer to a plate, pile the *rucola* in the middle of the *frittata* and drizzle on the pesto.

DEEP FRIED ZUCCHINI FLOWERS WITH TASMANIAN GRUYERE

SERVES 6 AS A FIRST COURSE

Ingredients

200 g plain flour

2/3 cup cold water

24 zucchini flowers

250 g 'Heidi' Tasmanian gruyere, grated (Fontina will do)

olive oil for deep frying

salt and pepper to taste

Method

To make the batter, mix the flour and water together until they form a rough, lumpy mixture. Rest this while you are preparing the rest of the dish.

Trim the ends of the zucchini if the flowers have them attached. Now carefully open the ends of the flowers and fill them with a little of the grated cheese.

Heat the olive oil until it is about to smoke, then dip the filled zucchini flowers in the batter, allowing any excesses to run off. Fry the flowers in the oil until they are golden.

Take them out, season and serve with some garden greens.

SEARED CUTTLEFISH WITH SWEET ONIONS AND RUCOLA

SERVES 4 AS A FIRST COURSE

Ingredients

allow about 1 cuttlefish per person, cleaned, keep ink sac

sweet onions (Kunanurra), sliced thinly

extra virgin olive oil

rucola — as much as you like, washed and dried

salt and pepper

Method

Gently fry the onions with about 3 tablespoons of olive oil in a pan until they are soft and transparent. Season and set aside. Slice the cuttlefish into ½-cm-wide pieces about 4 cm long. Heat a little olive oil in a skillet until it is about to smoke. Drop in the cuttlefish pieces and sear at high heat, turning them, until they are golden brown on both sides. Season them well.

Presentation

Toss the *rucola* with some olive oil in a bowl, then use some of these dressed leaves as a base on the serving plate. Next put some of the onion then the cuttlefish on top. Serve immediately.

TAGLIATELLE WITH HARBOUR PRAWNS AND LEEKS

SERVES 8 AS A FIRST COURSE

For the sauce

Ingredients

prawn shells from 500 g cooked harbour prawns
   (keeping the meat for later)
2 celery sticks, cut into chunks
1 carrot, cut into rounds
2 leeks, chopped
6 ripe tomatoes, peeled and chopped
parsley, roughly chopped
1 additional leek
good olive oil (optional)

Method

Place the prawn shells, vegetables, tomatoes and parsley in a pot. Cover with plenty of cold fresh water and bring to a simmer. Keep simmering for 1–1½ hours then strain. Reduce until it is intense enough, then season to taste. To finish the sauce, thinly slice the additional leek and let it simmer gently for 2 minutes in the reduction. Add 2–3 tablespoons of good olive oil, if you wish, for richness and complexity.

Pasta and assembly

Follow the basic method for pasta (page 29) and cut the sheets into *tagliatelle*.

Bring a large pot of boiling water to the boil. Add a generous pinch of salt, then throw in the tagliatelle, a few at a time, so that the water does not lose its boil. Cook the pasta until it is *al dente*. Drain well, put it in a bowl, add the sauce and prawn meat and serve immediately.

PEACH AND GINGER DOME

A DESSERT THAT SERVES 8

The custard

Ingredients

200 g blanched almonds, finely chopped
1 vanilla bean, split and scraped
180 ml milk
40 g caster sugar
2 egg yolks
1 leaf gelatine, dissolved in water
75 ml whipped cream

Method

Bring the milk to the boil, add the almonds and vanilla bean and allow to infuse for 1 hour. Strain and make a *crema inglese* (see page 38), with sugar and yolks. Add the gelatine and mix thoroughly. Cool, then fold in the whipped cream and set aside.

The sponge

Ingredients

2 whole eggs
75 g sugar
40 g plain flour, sifted

Method

Cream the yolks and sugar until they are thick and fluffy. Fold in the flour. Spread onto a baking sheet and bake in a preheated oven at 180°C till just cooked. Cut to the size of the mould (a miniature brioche tin about 8 cm x 3 cm). Soak the sponge with the peach syrup (see below).

Peach syrup

Ingredients

1 cling stone peach, peeled and cut into thin slices
200 ml water
80 g sugar
1 vanilla bean, halved and scraped
1 tablespoon armagnac

Method

Simmer peach slices in the water with the sugar and vanilla until they are soft enough to mash. Remove the vanilla pod and mash the peaches in the liquid completely. Add the armagnac.

Ginger jelly

Ingredients

150 ml water
30 g sugar
50 g fresh ginger, peeled and finely grated
1 leaf gelatine, dissolved in a little cold water

Method

In a small saucepan bring the water, sugar and ginger to the boil and simmer for 1 minute until the sugar has dissolved. Add the gelatine and mix thoroughly. Pour about $\frac{1}{2}$ cm into the bases of the moulds.

The biscotti

Ingredients

100 g walnuts, roasted and roughly chopped
100 g almonds, roasted and roughly chopped
1 cup caster sugar
2 whole eggs
1/2 teaspoon baking powder
2 cups plain flour
1 egg white

Method

Blend sugar and eggs together, mix in the flour and baking powder gradually. Knead in a floured board with the nuts. Roll into a log and rest in the refrigerator briefly.

Then glaze with the egg white and bake in a preheated 110°C oven for 30–40 minutes. Now slice the log into thin rounds and return to the oven to dry. Cool, then chop roughly into large crumbs.

The dome

Ingredients

500 g sugar
150 ml water
2 tablespoons liquid glucose

Method

Cover the bottom of a small round mixing bowl (about 10 cm in diameter) with foil and oil lightly. Bring the sugar, water and glucose to a pale toffee (160°C). Dip the bowl in the toffee, allowing any excess to drain off. Cool, remove foil and toffee cover from bowl, then peel off the foil carefully with tweezers.

Assembly
ripe peaches, thinly sliced

Use individual, tiny brioche loaf tins (about 8 cm x 3 cm).

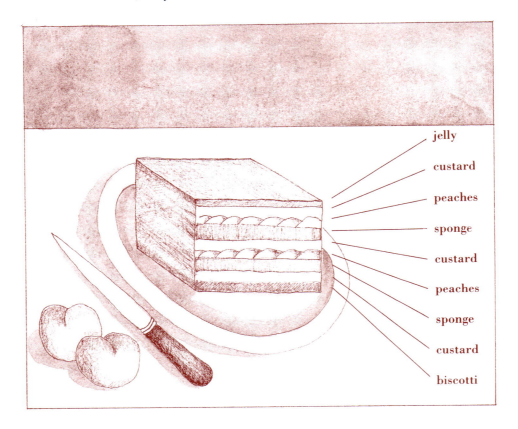

To serve, turn out the mould onto the serving plate, then cover with the dome and serve.

PEACH AND RASPBERRY SPONGE

MAKES 6 INDIVIDUAL SPONGES

The sponge

Ingredients

6 egg yolks
75 g caster sugar
6 egg whites
150 g caster sugar
80 g plain flour, sifted

Method

Cream the yolks and first amount of caster sugar until they are thick and fluffy. Whip the egg whites and second amount of sugar together until they form soft peaks. Now fold the two mixtures and the flour together. Spread onto two baking sheets at about 1 cm in depth and bake in a preheated oven at 180°C till just cooked. Cut the sponge into 18 equal rectangles.

Raspberry sorbet

MAKES 1 LITRE

Ingredients

500 ml pureed, sieved raspberries
400 ml sugar syrup

Method

Mix together, churn and freeze until needed.

Assembly

allow 1/2 large peach per person, sliced
caster sugar
1 cup fresh double cream

Layer the dessert, starting with sponge on the bottom, then some double cream, peach slices, sponge again, raspberry sorbet, and finish off with sponge dipped in caster sugar.

March to May

Vegetables

Asparagus
  (start of the Queensland season)
Snake beans
Wild mushrooms
  (saffron milkcaps or orange
  flycaps [*Lactarius deliciosus*],
  scotch bonnets [*Tricholoma
  terreum*], slippery jacks [*Suillus
  luteus*], pine boletus [*Boletus
  pulverulentus*]) towards the end
Broccoli
Cauliflower
Turnips
Beetroot
Fresh garlic
Corn
Queensland blue pumpkins
  (late summer/autumn)
Butternuts
Chinese or English spinach
Borlotti beans
  (late summer/autumn)
Brussels sprouts
Parsnips
Sugar snaps
Snow peas

Fruit

Blackberries
Raspberries
Blueberries (finishing)
Persimmons
Pomegranates
Quinces (best in March)
Figs
Tamarillos
Kiwi fruit
New season apples (Galas,
  new season Delicious; with
  apples especially, eat in season
  rather than the tired, stale,
  stored fruit of summer)
Nashi
Custard apples (these start in April)
Passionfruit
Avocados (the heaviest ones appear
in autumn)
Bananas (as for avocados)
End of the apricots (best in March)
Nectarines (finishing)
Mandarins (April)
Grapes
Peaches (finishing)
Pears
Plums (finishing, late bloods
  especially good)
Watermelon
Rockmelon

AUTUMN — MARCH TO MAY

Autumn begins warm in Sydney: not until the end of April or early May do we get anything comparable to a European autumn. Then we can start to forget the delicacy of summer and savour more robust flavours. As the chill creeps into the air, leave the crisp white wines behind and uncork the first of the warming reds: now begin the comfort foods.

I love the nourishment of rich clear broths in these weeks: duck, quail, and veal shank with borlotti beans. Now is the time for such earthy foods, for pigeon, venison, chestnuts, mushrooms. Especially mushrooms.

We drive to Oberon and scour the pine forests for wild mushrooms: saffron milkcaps, slippery jacks and scotch bonnets. Many of the European varieties grow here now, having come across as spore with the seedlings and saplings of the original pines. Once, I even found a truffle. It had no odour or flavour, but it was a truffle. In time, who knows?

The season suggests the flavours and the combinations: earthy, gamey flavours with root vegetables, the turnips and beetroots, and the first of the fresh garlic; quail with chestnuts and baby turnips; venison with wild mushrooms and braised leeks.

Now the pastas pick up rustic flavours, a *papardelle* with a hare sauce or *tagliatelle* with a rabbit and prosciutto sauce.

Tuna is excellent, as are the big-flavoured reef fish, red emperor, coral trout and sweetlip. Roast them in the oven and serve them with sturdy accompaniments like roasted garlic and anchovy *salsa*.

This is the season for pigeons from Wycheproof in Victoria: tender, rich with flavour, slightly gamey with dense dark flesh. I use the late Genoa black figs to accompany the roast birds.

When the second crop of asparagus comes in, we serve it in the Veronese style, with poached egg, olive oil and shaved parmesan.

And fruit: the last of the mangoes, the berries — loganberries, raspberries, blueberries and currants — quinces (best in March) and new season apples. This is the best season for fruit.

AUTUMN RECIPES

Pigeon and black fig salad
*Grilled Coffin Bay scallops in their shells with prosciutto,
parsley and garlic*
*Barbecued duck with braised radicchio heart
in balsamic vinegar*
Fried sea scallops with a bollito of beetroot and onion
Roast venison cutlet with Chinese mushrooms and polenta
Chocolate and nougat tartufo
Rare roast beef and linguini salad
Barbecued vegetables with Jerusalem artichoke puree
Vanilla and chocolate cassata with spiced quinces
Fish and shellfish broth with roast garlic crostini
Yamba prawn cutlets with a garlic maionese
Braised zucchini in white wine, parsley and garlic
Poached reef fish with braised zucchini
Quail and pine boletus broth
Roast orange flycaps with garlic and parsley
Pigeon and shiitake salad
Tagliatelle with wild mushroom sauce
Salad of pan fried chicken livers, parmesan and pasta triangles
Grilled figs with mascarpone
Mascarpone
Little fig and mascarpone tarts with crema inglese
Data and macadamia nut cake

AUTUMN — MARCH TO MAY

AUTUMN MENU

Fish and shellfish broth with roast garlic crostini
Pigeon and black fig salad
Roast venison cutlet with Chinese mushrooms and polenta
Chocolate and nougat tartufo

Grilled Coffin Bay scallops in their shells with prosciutto,
parsley and garlic
Barbecued vegetables with Jerusalem artichoke puree
Barbecued duck with braised radicchio heart
in balsamic vinegar
Vanilla and chocolate cassata with spiced quinces

Quail and pine boletus broth
Fried sea scallops with a bollito of beetroot and onion
Poached reef fish with braised zucchini
Grilled figs with mascarpone

Rare roast beef and linguini salad
Tagliatelle with wild mushroom sauce
Salad of pan fried chicken livers, parmesan and pasta triangles
Little fig and mascarpone tarts with crema inglese

Pigeon and shiitake salad
Yamba prawn cutlets with a garlic maionese
Braised zucchini in white wine, parsley and garlic
Roast orange flycaps with garlic and parsley
Date and macadamia nut cake

PIGEON AND BLACK FIG SALAD

SERVES 6 AS A FIRST COURSE

Ingredients
3 pigeons, trimmed at the wings and neck
extra virgin olive oil
freshly ground pepper
1 head young curly endive, cleaned and cut into pieces
red wine vinegar
6 ripe, soft, black figs
veal stock
seasoning to taste

Method
Preheat oven to 240°C. Place the pigeons in a baking dish, rub with olive oil and season with pepper. Roast for 10–12 minutes, keeping the pigeons quite pink. Take out of the oven and rest for a further 10 minutes.

Take the breasts off the bone, remove the legs and make them into a salad with the endive, olive oil and vinegar.

Cut the figs in half and warm them in the veal stock. Sprinkle some of the olive oil into the stock. Season and arrange the figs, together with the salad, on plates. Pour a little of the hot sauce over each salad and serve.

GRILLED COFFIN BAY SCALLOPS IN THEIR SHELLS WITH PROSCIUTTO, PARSLEY AND GARLIC

SERVES 6 AS A FIRST COURSE

Ingredients

36 Coffin Bay scallops in their shells, cleaned

12 thin slices prosciutto, cut into small thin strips

6 cloves garlic, minced

1 handful parsley, chopped fine

6 tablespoons extra virgin olive oil

salt and pepper to taste

Method

Preheat the oven to 250°C. Arrange the scallops on oven trays. In each scallop put some prosciutto strips, garlic, parsley and a little of the olive oil. Season and place in the oven until the scallops are sizzling. Should take 10–12 minutes. Serve with a salad of young garden greens.

BARBECUED DUCK WITH BRAISED RADICCHIO HEART IN BALSAMIC VINEGAR

SERVES 6 AS A MAIN COURSE

Ingredients

3 x size 23–25 Peking-Aylesbury cross ducks

6 radicchio hearts, trimmed of all the tough outer leaves

450 g snow peas, cleaned

1 litre veal stock

balsamic vinegar

extra virgin olive oil

salt

Method

To prepare the duck, remove the legs and the entire rib cage. Trim the wings off at the first joint. Cut through the breast bone separating the two breasts, but leave them on the bone.

Salt the skin on the breast and leg pieces well; place them skin side down in a roasting pan and place in a hot 250°C preheated oven for 12–15 minutes. This will crisp the skin as well as removing most of the fat so that the duck pieces are ready for the barbecue.

Once the duck pieces are on the barbecue or char grill, the radicchio hearts can be simmered in the veal stock until they are tender. Blanch the snow peas in boiling water, drain and distribute evenly among the serving plates. Place a radicchio heart on top of the snow peas and dress with a little of the extra virgin olive oil.

Take each duck breast off the bone, slice into 5–6 pieces, arrange on the plates next to the radicchio and the snow peas. Finally cut the leg at the joint, add to the rest and sprinkle with the balsamic vinegar. Serve immediately.

FRIED SEA SCALLOPS WITH A BOLLITO OF BEETROOT AND ONION

SERVES 6 AS A MAIN COURSE

The bollito

Ingredients

3–4 medium–large beetroot, tops off

6–8 medium white or brown onions, skin left on

extra virgin olive oil

salt and pepper to taste

Method

In a large pot cover the beetroot and onions with cold water and bring to the boil. Turn the heat down to a simmer until the vegetables are cooked. Peel the beetroot and cut into thick wedges. Squeeze out the middles of the onions and discard the skin. Dress with the olive oil and season to taste.

The scallops

Ingredients

olive oil

allow about 12 sea scallops per person

6 cloves garlic, minced

salt and pepper to taste

Method

Heat the olive oil in a skillet until it begins to smoke. Add the scallops and fry on both sides until they are golden brown. Add the minced garlic and fry a little more. Season and serve with the *bollito*.

ROAST VENISON CUTLET WITH CHINESE MUSHROOMS AND POLENTA

SERVES 6 AS A MAIN COURSE

The mushrooms

Ingredients

1 kg wood fungus and oyster mushrooms

1 large onion, roughly chopped

1 leek, sliced

4 cloves garlic, minced

1/2 cup veal stock

olive oil

large handful parsley, chopped

salt and pepper

Method

Chop the mushrooms into bite-size pieces.

Place the onion, leek and garlic in a pot with some olive oil and fry gently. Add the mushrooms and stir continuously at high heat until they soften. Add the veal stock and bring to the boil. Simmer for about 15 minutes then add the parsley and season.

Soft polenta

Ingredients
1.5 litres salted water
250 g coarse polenta flour
handful freshly grated parmesan

Method
Bring the salted water to the boil then slowly add the polenta, stirring constantly with a wooden spoon or whisk until the polenta comes away from the sides of the saucepan. Turn down to a simmer and place a lid on. Simmer for about 20 minutes, giving the polenta a good stir every 5 minutes. The polenta should be soft and tender, ready for serving.

The venison

Ingredients
allow 1 cutlet per person
cracked black pepper
olive oil
soft polenta (see above)
Chinese mushrooms (see above)

Method
Preheat oven to 160°C. Sprinkle each cutlet with the cracked black pepper. Heat some olive oil in a frypan and seal each cutlet. Transfer to the oven and roast for 12–15 minutes. Rest for a further 10 minutes then serve with the polenta and mushrooms.

CHOCOLATE AND NOUGAT TARTUFO

MAKES ABOUT 16 INDIVIDUAL TARTUFI

Gelato base

Ingredients

1.5 litres single cream
200 g honey
100 g sugar
12 egg yolks

Method

Cook as for *crema inglese* (page 38) to 80°C then cool and churn.

Chocolate cream

Ingredients

300 g best quality milk chocolate, cut into small pieces
200 ml single cream

Method

Bring the cream to the boil. Remove it from the heat, whisk in the chocolate, then set aside to cool.

The dry mix

Ingredients

4 cups coconut threads
1/2 cup whole raw blanched peanuts
1/2 cup whole raw almonds
750 g hard Italian torrone (nougat) (Flamigni is excellent),
    cut into small, rough dice

Method

Roast the coconut, peanuts and almonds in a slow 100°–120°C oven until they have browned slightly. Set aside to cool.

Coconut custard

Ingredients

1 cup of the roasted coconut threads (see above)
1200 ml single cream
8 egg yolks
200 g sugar

Method

Add the coconut to the cream, bring to the boil and set aside for 30 minutes to infuse. Strain through a cloth then proceed as with a *crema inglese* (page 38) with the yolks and the sugar. Set aside to cool.

Assembly and serving

Add 2 cups of the roasted coconut and the rest of the dry mix ingredients to the chocolate cream and mix thoroughly. Add to the gelato and mix. Spoon the mixture into small individual moulds and freeze overnight.

To serve, unmould, roll each *tartufo* in the remaining coconut and serve with the coconut custard.

RARE ROAST BEEF AND LINGUINI SALAD

SERVES 6 AS A FIRST COURSE

Ingredients

600–700 g piece of beef butt fillet
linguini (basic pasta page 29)
caper salsa (page 108)
olive oil
salt and pepper

Method

Preheat oven to 250°C. Rub the butt fillet with olive oil and season with freshly ground black pepper. Place the beef in a baking dish and roast for 10–12 minutes. Take from the oven and rest for at least 30 minutes.

Put the *linguini* in a bowl and add the caper dressing; toss, taste for seasoning, then serve with the thinly sliced beef.

BARBECUED VEGETABLES WITH JERUSALEM ARTICHOKE PUREE

SERVES 6 AS A FIRST COURSE

The puree

Ingredients

2 kg Jerusalem artichokes, peeled
50 g butter
4 tablespoons extra virgin olive oil
salt and pepper to taste

Method

Place the Jerusalem artichokes in a pot and cover with cold water. Cover with the lid, bring to the boil then simmer for 15 minutes until the artichokes are tender. Drain off all the water.

Place the hot artichokes in a food processor with the butter and blend, slowly dribbling in the olive oil until the artichokes are pureed. Season and place in a bowl until needed.

The vegetables

Ingredients

1 medium eggplant, cut into 6 pieces each about 1 cm thick
1 red capsicum, sliced into 6 from top to bottom
6 field mushrooms, stems trimmed
6 spring onions, trimmed of their outer skin
1 medium red sweet potato, sliced into 6 pieces about 1 cm thick
6 small to medium zucchini
1/4 cup extra virgin olive oil
salt and pepper

Method

Salt the sliced eggplant on both sides and leave for about 15 minutes. The salt will help to extract the bitterness that appears on its surface in the form of moisture. Pat the eggplant gently with a teatowel or absorbent paper. Brush the eggplant with olive oil; it is now ready to barbecue.

The capsicum and mushrooms should also be brushed with olive oil and seasoned to prepare them for cooking.

Plunge the spring onions, sweet potato and zucchini into boiling salted water briefly until they are just cooked but still *al dente*. These should also then be lightly brushed with olive oil. Slice zucchini and spring onions in half from top to bottom, season, then place on the barbecue and grill on each side together with the eggplant, capsicum and mushrooms.

Serve with Jerusalem artichoke puree either at room temperature or hot.

VANILLA AND CHOCOLATE CASSATA WITH SPICED QUINCES

SERVES 6–10 AS DESSERT

Spiced quinces

Ingredients

2 quinces, peeled and sliced

375 ml sweet wine such as moscato, botrytis affected riesling, semillon or the like

150 g sugar

1 quill cassia bark

Method

In a baking dish lay out the slices of quince, add the sweet wine and sprinkle the sugar on top. Add the cassia bark making sure it is in the liquid. Cover with foil and bake very slowly at about 100°C for 3 hours. The quinces should be a rich tawny burgundy colour and tender in texture. Allow to cool before using.

For the cassata...

Chocolate gelato
Ingredients
185 g sugar
8 egg yolks
1 litre single cream
1 tablespoon cocoa, completely dissolved in a little milk

Method
Beat sugar and egg yolks together until they are pale.

Heat the cream almost to the boil. Don't boil. Whisk in the egg–sugar mixture. Place on a low heat and stir continuously with a wooden spoon until the mixture thickens and coats the spoon. Add the chocolate, then cool completely before churning.

Vanilla gelato
Ingredients
160 sugar
8 egg yolks
1 litre single cream
1 vanilla bean, sliced lengthways and scraped into the cream before heating

Method
Beat sugar and egg yolks together until they are pale.

Heat the cream almost to the boil. Don't boil. Whisk in the egg-sugar mixture. Place on a low heat and stir continuously with a wooden spoon until the mixture thickens and coats the spoon. Cool completely before churning.

Chocolate sorbetto
Ingredients
60 g cocoa
250 ml water
250 g sugar
1 tablespoon ground cassia
1 vanilla bean, halved and scraped

Method
Add the cocoa to about 50 ml of the water and whisk until all the cocoa has been dissolved completely.

Place all the ingredients in a saucepan, bring to the boil and simmer for 2–3 minutes until all the sugar has dissolved.

Cool before churning. Once churned, make a log with the *sorbetto* by wrapping it with aluminium foil approximately the length of your *cassata* mould, then placing it into the freezer to set till needed.

Assembling the cassata
Spoon the chocolate *gelato* into the *cassata* mould so that it comes one third of the way up. (A terrine mould can be used for this purpose.)

Cut the chocolate *sorbetto* log to the length of the mould and place it in the middle, on top of the chocolate *gelato*, lengthways.

After each of these first two steps it will be necessary to rest the partially completed *cassata* in the freezer for 2 hours before continuing.

Now fill the rest of the space with the vanilla *gelato*, cover with the lid and allow to set for at least 3 hours.

To serve, unmould by enclosing the entire mould with a warm, wet towel. Turn the *cassata* out onto a tray and slice as needed. Serve with some of the baked quinces.

FISH AND SHELLFISH BROTH WITH ROAST GARLIC CROSTINI

SERVES 8–10 AS A FIRST COURSE

Ingredients

fish and shellfish broth (page 24)
8 slices day-old focaccia, about 1 cm thick and 5–6 cm long
1 whole bulb garlic

Method

Place the slices of *focaccia* on a baking tray and brush each side lightly with olive oil. Place in a slow oven (about 100–120°C) for about 10 minutes until the bread has lightly toasted. Remove and allow to cool.

Now roast the whole garlic bulb at 150°C for 20–30 minutes until it has completely softened inside. Remove from the oven and allow to cool for 10 minutes. With a sharp knife slice $^1/_2$ cm off the top of the bulb, exposing the creamy centre of the cloves. Squeeze the bulb so that the creamy roast flesh oozes out easily.

Mix in a tablespoon of olive oil with this flesh, then spread a little on each of the *crostini* as you would butter.

To serve the broth, ladle into bowls then float the *crostini* on top.

YAMBA PRAWN CUTLETS WITH A GARLIC MAIONESE

Food, like everything else, is subject to the whims of fashion. Dishes pop in and out of favour, but we shouldn't let this affect our choices. Prawn cutlets may have become rather 'down-market', but when you cook them yourself, using succulent Yamba prawns from the north coast of New South Wales, and dunk them in a garlic maionese, memories of restaurant fare recede into the distance.

SERVES 4 AS A FIRST COURSE

Ingredients

16 Yamba prawns, shelled, tails left on and butterflied
1 egg, beaten
1 cup bread crumbs
1/4 cup olive oil
salt and pepper
8 tablespoons garlic maionese* (see below)

Method

Crumb the cutlets by lightly flouring each of them, dipping in the beaten egg and finally rolling in the crumbs. Heat some olive oil in a skillet and fry each side of the cutlets lightly until they are golden. Season and serve immediately with the garlic *maionese*.

Garlic maionese

MAKES ABOUT 1 1/4 CUPS

Ingredients

3 egg yolks
1/2 cup light olive oil
1/2 cup extra virgin olive oil
4–5 cloves garlic, mashed
1 tablespoon water
2 tablespoons lemon juice
salt and pepper

Method

Place the egg yolks in a bowl and whisk until they are smooth. Start to dribble the oil in a little at a time and keep whisking until it has all been incorporated. Now whisk in the mashed garlic, then the lemon juice. Season with salt and pepper. The water should be used at this point to correct the texture to your liking. If you like a firm *maionese*, then no water is needed. If you prefer a softer texture, then whisk in the water.

---

* Garlic *maionese* should be used within two days because the garlic flavour tends to change after that time. The oil used in this *maionese* is really up to you. For the extra virgin olive oil a lighter, more subtle oil from Liguria will give you a softer, finer flavoured *maionese*. Tuscany and Umbria produce peppery, more robust oils resulting in a richer, fuller flavoured *maionese*.

BRAISED ZUCCHINI IN WHITE WINE, PARSLEY AND GARLIC

SERVES 6 AS A SIDE DISH OR AS AN ACCOMPANIMENT TO POACHED FISH

Ingredients

6 tablespoons olive oil

1 onion, cut into chunks

500 g zucchini, cut into 1-cm-thick chunks

1/2 cup dry white wine

3 cloves garlic, chopped together with the parsley

large handful Italian parsley, chopped with the garlic

1 large tomato, seeded and chopped

salt and pepper

Method

Place the oil in a saucepan, then the onions, then the zucchini in that order. Turn the flame up high. When it starts to sizzle, wait one minute then stir well. Cook for another 3–4 minutes, stirring continuously.

Add the wine, garlic and parsley, and the tomato. Stir, cooking for 2–3 minutes more. Take the zucchini off the heat, season then rest for at least 15 minutes.

Note The oil is not heated initially here. It is also important that the onion start off between the oil and the zucchini as it takes just a little longer to cook. This process minimises the amount of water released by the zucchini and retains a slight crunchiness in their texture.

POACHED REEF FISH WITH BRAISED ZUCCHINI

SERVES 4 AS A MAIN COURSE

Ingredients

1½ litres fish or shellfish stock (page 24)
8 scaloppine cut from the fillet of a reef fish, about 1.5 cm thick
salt and pepper
braised zucchini (page 175)

Method

Place the fish stock in a baking dish, preferably ceramic. Arrange the pieces of reef fish in the dish, season with salt and pepper and place in a preheated oven at 220°C for about 10 minutes, until the fish is barely cooked in the middle. Serve immediately on top of the braised zucchini.

QUAIL AND PINE BOLETUS BROTH

SERVES 6–8 AS A FIRST COURSE

Ingredients

quail bones, roasted lightly
carrot, onion, celery, garlic, leek, chopped into 2-cm chunks
pine boletus mushrooms*
seasoning
grated parmesan

Method

Put quails and vegetables in a pot large enough to hold everything comfortably. Cover with cold water, bring to the boil, then simmer gently for at least 1½ hours. Strain and reduce if not intense enough. Slice the boletus mushrooms and simmer for 5–10 minutes in the broth. Season and serve immediately with freshly grated parmesan.

---

* The mushrooms need to be peeled because the skin on the cap is very sticky. The sponge under the cap also needs to be removed. The only usable part is the yellow flesh.

ROAST ORANGE FLYCAPS WITH GARLIC AND PARSLEY

SERVES 4 AS A FIRST COURSE

Ingredients

12 small, whole orange flycaps
1 onion or leek, sliced thin
handful grated parmesan cheese
handful chopped parsley
3 cloves minced garlic
3 tablespoons breadcrumbs
extra virgin olive oil

Method

Cut the stems from the mushrooms and mince the stems together with the onion and garlic. Fry the mixture gently in olive oil. Mix with the parmesan, breadcrumbs and garlic.

Fill each little cap with the mixture and bake in a 200°C preheated oven for 10 minutes.

PIGEON AND SHIITAKE SALAD

SERVES 4 AS A MAIN COURSE

Ingredients

4 pigeons, heads removed, wings removed to the first joint
rucola leaves
600 g shiitake mushrooms
virgin olive oil
balsamic vinegar
salt and vinegar

Method

Place pigeons and mushrooms in a baking dish, sprinkle with olive oil, season and roast for about 20 minutes in a hot oven (220°C) until fairly rare. Rest for another 20 minutes. After resting, slice the breast, legs and thighs. Place the pigeon pieces, mushrooms and *rucola* in a bowl and dress with virgin olive oil and balsamic vinegar. Season and serve.

TAGLIATELLE WITH WILD MUSHROOM SAUCE

SERVES 8 AS A FIRST COURSE

Sauce

Ingredients

1 kg wild mushrooms (e.g. ceps, orange flycaps, slippery jacks)

1 large onion, roughly chopped

1 leek, sliced

4 cloves garlic, minced

large handful parsley, chopped

1/2 cup dry white wine

olive oil

salt and pepper

600 g tagliatelle (see basic pasta recipe, page 29)

Method

Chop the mushrooms into bite-size pieces.

Place the onion, leek and garlic in a pot with some olive oil and fry gently. Add the mushrooms and stir continuously at high heat until they soften. Add the wine and bring to the boil.

Simmer for about 15 minutes then add the parsley and season.

Cook the tagliatelle in plenty of salted water and toss with the sauce.

SALAD OF PAN FRIED CHICKEN LIVERS WITH PARMESAN AND PASTA TRIANGLES

SERVES 6 AS A FIRST COURSE

Ingredients

400 g chicken livers, trimmed
8 pieces thinly sliced prosciutto
pasta triangles coated in grated parmesan (see note below)
garden greens , rucola, lamb's lettuce, mizuna, or the like
extra virgin olive oil
balsamic vinegar
salt and pepper

Method

Sear the chicken livers in a pan with some olive oil, season and reserve. In the same pan fry the prosciutto very quickly until it is crisp. Dress the greens with olive oil and balsamic vinegar and assemble the livers, triangles and prosciutto on top.

Note   To make the triangles, roll the pasta from the basic recipe (page 29), leaving it a little thicker. Now cut the triangles, with 3-cm sides, and cook as you would ordinary pasta. Place in cold water to cool. Remove from the water, coat with grated parmesan and lightly fry in a little olive oil until golden and slightly crisp.

GRILLED FIGS WITH MASCARPONE

Ingredients

allow 2–2 1/2 figs per person, according to size
caster sugar
fresh mascarpone (page 180)

Method
Cut the figs in half, top to bottom, and lay them down, cut side up. Sprinkle gradually with caster sugar while applying the heat of a domestic blowtorch. When the sugar has turned a golden caramel colour, plate and serve with the mascarpone.

MASCARPONE

Ingredients
1 litre double cream
1/4 teaspoon tartaric acid

Method
Heat the cream to 70°C. Ladle about half a cup of the hot cream into a bowl and whisk in the tartaric acid until it is completely dissolved. Mix this into the rest of the heated cream and leave in a bowl to set.

It will start to set after 10–15 minutes at which time it should be placed in enough muslin so that it can be completely enclosed. The muslin containing the cream should be placed in a sieve and this in turn placed over a bowl to catch the separating water. Place the entire contraption in the refrigerator for about 12 hours (overnight).

The resulting mascarpone stays fresh for about two days after which it will take on a slight tang. It should then be used for cooking.

Fresh, sweet mascarpone can be used as an accompaniment for figs or other fresh fruit such as berries. It can also be used for filling tart shells in place of crème patissiere.

LITTLE FIG AND MASCARPONE TARTS WITH CREMA INGLESE

MAKES ABOUT 12 TARTS

Pastry

Ingredients

325 g flour, sifted
250 g butter
125 g caster sugar
60 ml cold water

Method

Sift flour onto board. Add sugar. Use the large holes on a cheese grater to grate the cold butter on to the flour and sugar. Mix quickly. Butter strands won't disappear. Add cold water.

Form pastry into a log for cutting circles from later. Rest for 1 hour in refrigerator.

Cut off slices as needed and roll on a floured board. Roll into tartlet shells and trim around edges. Rest for 10 minutes then bake at 180°C till golden.

Crema inglese

Ingredients

250 ml milk
250 ml single cream
1 vanilla bean, cut in half lengthways
5 egg yolks
120 g sugar

Method

Heat milk, cream and vanilla bean to just below boiling. Beat yolks and sugar until they are pale and form a ribbon. Add the hot liquid and mix thoroughly. Transfer to a saucepan over low heat, stirring constantly. The *crema* is done when it coats the back of the spoon.

Assembly

Allow 2 figs per person, sliced, and 2 tablespoons mascarpone for each tart. You will need a little cream to soften the mascarpone if it is too thick.

Fill the tarts with mascarpone. Arrange the fig slices evenly on top. Serve with a small jug of *crema inglese*.

DATE AND MACADAMIA NUT CAKE

MAKES ONE 25-CM CAKE

Ingredients

4 eggs
250 g self-raising flour
250 g softened butter
250 g brown sugar
4 drops vanilla essence
350 g dates, chopped into quarters
4 tablespoons macadamia nut pieces

Method

Cream the butter and sugar in an electric beater. While still beating at low speed, drop in the vanilla and add the flour slowly. Turn up the speed on the beater and add the eggs one at a time until they are incorporated. Fold in the dates and macadamia nuts.

Butter and flour a 25-cm cake tin and spoon the mixture into this. Bake in a preheated oven at 170°C for 40 minutes, then drop to 150°C until set (when the top of the cake springs back to the touch).

WINE

So much is written and talked about wine, yet so often a simple and central maxim is forgotten. Wine is about food, and food is mostly about wine. It's the one statement you could make anywhere in Europe on the subject without disagreement. Culturally, they cohabit. Have the various wine styles developed because of the food eaten, or have the wines dictated the style of food eaten? Who knows? One is inextricably interwoven with the other — and with climate, naturally.

As an Italian who grew up in predominantly Anglo-Saxon Australia, I'm aware of the differing approach of these two cultures to wine. The American approach, perhaps an extreme example of the Anglo-Saxon analytical tendency, was outlined by the Marchese Piero Antinori of the house of Antinori in Chianti.

When an American decides to be interested in wine, observed the Marchese, he buys books, goes to tastings and auctions, and buys and tastes as many wines as he can. Then, at the end of this exhaustive process, he will feel that he is ready to drink wine with his food. The Italians and the French grow up with wine on the table at every meal.

To extend this underlying principle, it follows that if you are to taste wine properly, you must take it with food — with the kind of food that best complements that wine.

This is the problem I have with wine shows and gold medals. Once, while visiting a winemaker in the Hunter, I was poured a glass of his world-famous chardonnay. It was heavy with gold and, to my mind, practically undrinkable, at least with food: it was far too woody. When I told him this, far from throwing me out, he agreed, producing another bottle which was, he said, the wine he made to drink himself. It was beautiful. The dilemma with show wines is, first, the wines are drunk seriously and without food, and second, nobody can taste that many and not be affected. In the end, the enormous tastes win all the medals because they cut through jaded palates. The lesson is, don't be dazzled by all that gold.

We Australians have taken to wine drinking and winemaking with astonishing rapidity and avidity. Our per capita consumption has outstripped the other Anglo-Saxon countries; we're 20th in ranking in the wine-consuming countries, behind Germany, ahead of New Zealand at 21, the United Kingdom at 26 and the USA at 29. Wine is our fastest growing agricultural export. And now, as the next stage in that process, we are beginning to make more and more of what I call balanced wines. Let me explain.

The full flavours of Australia's wines are related to the climate: a hotter climate produces more sugar in the grapes, and so we produce many wines where fruit is the predominant taste. I've drunk award-winning Coonawarra reds whose first taste on the palate is Ribena: I'm not too sure what to eat with that. Also, to my palate, many of those oak forest chardonnays and 'cat's piss' sauvignon blancs are merely unbalanced.

By balance, I mean structure: the fruit, the alcohol, the tannin and the acid are in balance, producing the quality called, by wine writers, vinosity. This means a taste, not like fruit juice, not like a carpenter's shop, but like wine.

Fortunately, at time of writing, Australian winemakers are beginning to produce more and more of these wines — good, honest wines, made to be drunk and enjoyed with food and not as overblown monuments to their makers. I would mention Andrew Pirie, Brian Croser and John Middleton among them. At his Mount Mary vineyard in the Yarra Valley, John Middleton produces what he calls a Sauvignon, a blend of sauvignon blanc and muscadet, which is steely, almost neutral in flavour. We serve it with oysters, an ideal combination. You simply can't drink one of those full-blown chardonnays with oysters: the chemical reaction between the iodine and the wood produces a horrible taste. And this brings us to the combinations of wine with food.

In the Amanusa resort in Bali recently I ate very good Thai food (cooked by an Australia!) — green curry and a coconut-based squid dish — with a chilled bottle of Andrew Pirie's unwooded pinot noir. It worked perfectly. The sweetness in the Thai food caught the sweet flavours of the pinot and, because there was no overlaying of wood, it was an ideal match. For every rule made, there is an exception. Blanket rules don't work, and the most important thing to remember is that half the fun is in trying to find new and unusual combinations. To do this, you must experiment. But where to start?

As an Australian, I grew up without a wine culture behind me. Yes, we drank wine at home, but it's not quite the same as growing up with the taste of your own regional wine on your dummy. Here is what I suggest for any Australian wondering where to start in learning an appreciation of wine.

First, start with Australian wines. Second, start with your local wines — if you're from Sydney, begin with the Hunter. From Adelaide, you have a wider choice, but pick one region. Get to know the flavours of the wines of that region, what wines go with what foods, what you like, and what you don't like.

Begin with the cheaper wines. Begin tentatively, as you would an affair; don't rush in and try everything all at once. Try a couple of rieslings, a few chardonnays, cabernet sauvignons, until you know the distinctive tastes of the variety. Your region may specialise in one variety; get to know that one especially.

Listen to your friends. Listen to what other people are recommending. Cultivate a wine merchant who seems to know what he's talking about. Try his recommendations. If you don't like them, tell him. Don't be afraid of this. You don't have to use wine words; they're for the poor professionals who have to suffer through tastings. You only have to come up with words to describe the taste so that you remember it. If it tastes like a forest just after the rain or dog piss or wet hessian, for you, that's it.

As you gain confidence and begin to develop your own tastes, start to pay a little more, move into an adjacent or different region, look for the smaller labels whose winemakers are more likely to be experimenting. (They have more failures too; often, if a batch is spoiled, a boutique winery can't afford to throw it out — but that's all part of the learning process.)

The matter of price is interesting. I'm lucky enough to be in a profession where it matters less, but I have noticed this: there are more wines asking top price that aren't worth it than there are at the cheaper end of the market. Also, note that the tendency of the larger companies is to make mass appeal wines; with some notable exceptions, they take fewer risks.

Because I grew up here, I began my journey of discovery with Australian wines, then, because of my heritage, moved into the Italians. The Italian experience in the last twenty years is worth recording.

Anybody drinking Italian wine before the 1980s could be excused for thinking it was, at best, good on the day, at worst generally poor. There were always heavenly exceptions: specific vintages of Barolos from good producers, for example, and some distinctive chianti.

What has happened was that, in the 1960s, the Italian government imposed a *Denominazione di Origine Controllata* in order to instil some order and quality into what was a fairly anarchic industry. The problem was that this also restricted those makers who wanted to experiment, and couldn't within the strict rules of the DOC. If you were making wine in the Chianti zone, for example, you had to use a fixed percentage of the *sangiovese* grape.

The winemakers who wanted to bend the rules came up with a creative solution to the problem. Outside the DOC restrictions were wines called *vino da tavola* — table wines — a classification meant for very ordinary everyday wines. So while you had an overall improvement in quality with the introduction of the DOC, the truly exceptional Italian wines, *Sassicaia* and Antinori's *Tignanello* for example, were to be found under the lowly *vino da tavola* classification.

Most Italian wine was so ordinary for so long because there was no need to export and, perhaps, because Italians would rather drink their wine than talk about it: if it was a little acid, *fa niente*? That's the way we make it. But the demands of the late twentieth century and the opportunities of the export market have changed that attitude enormously.

Only now, having worked my way through Australian and Italian wines, am I beginning to explore the French. But wine *is* made, not to be studied, not be pondered over, not to be bought and sold, but to be enjoyed. I find the notion of hanging on to a bottle of wine until it is vinegar, because to open it would be to lower its value, obscene. I can't keep wine. What's the point? In fact, as I get older, I'm enjoying wine a lot younger, especially the wonderful, brash young reds, full of sap and tannin. When I was young I had a thing about old reds that was approaching necrophilia. Reverentially, we would pull the cork on a decrepit old wine and be excited to find in it some vestige of its former glory.

Finally, I'm pleased to record a recent development in the winemaking regions, places like the Clare Valley, the Barossa and the Yarra, and that is the mingling of winemaking with cooking. Restaurants are opening to cater for, among others, the winemakers and their staff, using regional food, developing regional dishes. Fine cooks and winemakers are eating and drinking together. And we come back to the beginning — wine and food: food and wine.

BIBLIOGRAPHY

Antolini, Piero *Andar per Buon Olio*, Massimo Baldini, 1988.
Arcigola *Vini d'Italia*, Gamero Rosso, 1987.
Belfrage, Nicholas *Life beyond Lambrusco*, Sidgwick & Jackson, 1985.
Bertolli, Paul with Alice Waters *Chez Panisse Cooking*, Random House, 1988.
Bozzi, Ottorina Perna *La Lombardia in Cucina*, Giunti Martello, 1982.
Bugialli, Giuliano *The Fine Art of Italian Cooking*, Times Books, 1977.
Capnist, Giovanni *La Cucina Polesana*, Franco Muzzio, 1985.
Capozzi, Ave Ninchi E Pino *Il Riso*, Arnaldo Mondadori, 1976.
Castelvetro, Giacomo *The Fruit, Herbs and Vegetables of Italy*, Viking, 1989.
Davidson, Alan *Mediterranean Seafood*, Penguin, 1972.
Ferguson, Jenny *Cooking for You & Me*, Methuen Haynes, 1987.
Field, Carol *The Italian Baker*, Harper & Row, 1985.
Field, Carol *Celebrating Italy*, Morrow, 1990.
Giudi, Elena *Ricette d'Autore*, Rizzoli, 1983.
Halliday, James *The Australian Wine Compendium*, Angus & Robertson, 1985.
Isaacs, Jennifer *Bush Food — Aboriginal Food and Herbal Medicine*, Weldon, 1987.

Marchesi, Gualtiero *La Mia Nuova Grande Cucina Italiana*, Rizzoli, 1980.

Menichetti, Piero and Luciana Menichetti *Vecchia Cucina Eugubina*, Panfili Ikuvium, 1984.

Montani, Sandra and Anita Veroni *La Cucina della Bassa Padana*, Franco Muzzio, 1986.

Pirovano, Carlo (ed.) *Modern Italy — Images and History of a National Identity*, Electra Editrice, 1984.

Olszewski, Peter *A Salute to the Humble Yabby*, Angus & Robertson, 1980.

Santolini, Antonella *Umbria in Bocca*, Il Vespro, 1978.

GLOSSARY

al dente	cooked so that it still has texture
antipasto	coming before the meal; an appetizer
bocconcini	little balls of fresh mozzarella
bok choy	Chinese vegetable resembling the taste of Swiss chard, although sweeter in flavour
bollito	meaning 'boiled' in Italian
cannelloni	tubes of pasta with a filling
carpaccio	refers to raw meat or fish dish
cassata	refers to an ice-cream dessert made in a mould
cassia bark	the aromatic bark of the cassia tree
choy sum	Chinese flowering cabbage (yellow flowers)
corzetti	coin-shaped pasta
cotecchino	Italian pork sausage that has to be simmered in water
crema inglese	runny custard (*créme anglaise*)
crostini	toasts
een choy	Chinese spinach
focaccia	flat Italian bread
frittata	Italian omelette
frutta senapata	fruit preserved in sugar and mustard
gai lum	Chinese broccoli, has crisp dark leaves with small florets
gelato	ice-cream

grana	refers to the hard cheeses of Lombardy and Reggio Emilia
lamb's lettuce	small lamb's tongue shaped leaf, grows in clumps
lasagne	sheets of pasta with a filling between
lattughe	also called crostoli, chiacchiere, cenci, these little fried pastries are flavoured with grappa
linguini	long, flat pasta shape
maionese	mayonnaise
mascarpone	sweet dessert cream 'cheese'
mezzaluna	a 'half moon' shaped blade for chopping
millefoglia	'a thousand leaves'
mizuna	Japanese salad green, has a serrated leaf
momboli	Italian dialect word meaning meat taken from the lombo' or loin of the animal
pan di spagna	literally 'Spanish bread'; a firm sponge
pancetta	air-dried pork belly
panetonne	Italian fruit bread; a festive loaf
panforte	Siena specialty made from nuts, fruit and spices
passati	vegetables are cooked and then sieved
pasta frolla	shortcrust pastry
pasta sfoglio	puff pastry
pasta soffiata	choux pastry
pasta stracci	'rags' of pasta
peperonata	chunky braised capsicum, sweet onions, olive oil, garlic and basil
pesto	Genovese specialty made from basil, garlic and pine nuts
pizza	thin bread base with various toppings
polenta	like a porridge made from corn meal
porcini	'Boletus Edulus' mushrooms. Often found dried in Italian delis
prosciutto	air-dried leg of pork
radicchio	red Italian lettuce having a pleasant bitterness
ragu	mixture of meats, mushrooms or the like in a sauce or braise
risotto	northern Italian dish made from rice grown in that area

rotolo	a roll
rucola	also called rocket, ruchetta and arugola. Slightly peppery Italian salad green
salmi	usually meaning cooked in red wine and spices (cloves, cinnamon)
salsa	a thick sauce
salsa verde	made from parsley, garlic, anchovies, capers and olive oil
salsicce	sausages
scaloppine	thin slices
semifreddo	Italian soft ice cream (semi cold)
sformato	a moulded dish
soffiati	cream puffs made from choux pastry
sorbetto	sorbet or sherbet made from fruit puree, sugar and water
stracci	'rags' of pasta; the pasta sheet is cut into random lengths resembling rags
sugo	sauce
taslierini	thin strands of pasta. Thinner than spaghetti
tagliatelle	flat pasta strands usually about 1 cm wide
tartufo	truffle
torrone	nougat
tortelli	triangular-shaped filled pasta
tortelli di zucca	pumpkin-filled tortelli; specialty of the Brescia–Mantova area
vongole	baby clam
witlof	Belgian endive